MESSAGES

FROM~ANNA

Lessons in Living...
Santa Claus, God & Love

BY ZOE RANKIN

Health Communications, Inc.
Deerfield Beach, Florida

Zoe Rankin
Houston, Texas

Library of Congress Cataloging-in-Publication Data

Rankin, Zoe
    Messages from Anna.

        1. Conduct of life.   2. Rankin, Zoe
I. Title.
BJ1581.2.R367   1989   158'.1   88-28470
ISBN 1-55874-013-9

ISBN 1-55874-013-9

Published by: Health Communications, Inc.
                3201 S.W. 15th Street
                Deerfield Beach, Florida 33442

Cover design by Reta Thomas

FOREWORD

I have watched Zoe Rankin grow for twenty years. *Messages from Anna* is her flowering and blossoming. It's packed with wisdom!

T.S. Eliot gave us a mighty metaphor of modern life in his "pair of ragged claws scuttling across the floors of silent seas." Zoe offers us a solution in Anna's crab stories. This book will inspire us to shed our shells once and for all.

John E. Bradshaw

DEDICATED TO

Anna

THANKS TO

I want to thank those of you who survived as well as those who "let go" of me and my obsession during the writing of this book.

Beyond friendship and love three survivors were Nancy Sparks, Leona Fields and Stan Turner. Their breath kept alive my Santa, Anna, God and Love.

ACKNOWLEDGMENTS

I'm always impressed with an old friend's ability to understand another old friend's need for time and space. Some of these oldies I'd like to acknowledge are Red Barefield, Tom Cramer, Bob Geyer, Irina Langhans, Dolores Freeman, Terry Rambin, Cindy Kubecka, Linda Heck, Nancy Bradshaw, Sid Adger, Jimmy Curran, Betty Dreiss, Paige Jansen, Gail and Tex Brockett and Bill Price.

Nancy Geyer, Leone Hale and John Bradshaw, three authors I admire, gave to me their "gems" right along with some other professionals I'd like to mention, like Nolan Skipper, artist; Peggy Puckett, research consultant; Ty Webb, cover photographer; Judith Juhasz, my portrait photographer and everyone at Health Communications, especially Marie Stilkind.

To mention one person and not another seems unfair. There are so many including my Wednesday Daytime Group who have read my writings through the years and have encouraged me to continue. This page can't hold "all of you" but I hope my gift of Anna will say that I think of all of you.

Dear Reader,

"It's good to be a seeker but sooner or later you have to be a finder and then it is well to give what you have found, a gift into the world for whoever will accept it."

Richard Bach's words helped me to know that Anna was a gift worth sharing and that I need to quit seeking long enough to give you this gift.

Everyone in this book is real but most of them are living with a different name.

To leave an open, on-going linkage of thoughts with you is the only thing I can hope for with our limited time together. Anna said it best, "All I'll have when I die is what I've been able to give away and I have to give it away to keep it in my memory while I'm living."

Anna was 90 years old when we met in 1982.

In April, 1987, she went to Austin, Texas to select her own reading for the blind. Thrilled with her selection of Miltons' *Paradise Lost,* she quoted direct lines that she'd memorized as we talked. She gave to me her "Notebook for Living a Loving Life" and asked me to pass it on.

Perhaps I'll have another chance to share more of it with you.

Sincerely,
Zoe Rankin

CHAPTER
ONE

Ninety-year-old Anna took several tulip bulbs from a paper sack, instructing me as she threw them, "Dig the holes precisely where they fall. The tulips will look far more natural, and you can learn a most valuable lesson from the experience. Grow where you are planted! Life has a way of hurling us in all directions. Some of us grow and bloom while others complain and die. When I'm ready to die, I'll quit planting bulbs. Until then, I'll have something to look forward to in the springtime."

Wednesday, December 8, 1982

Meeting Anna

I had rented a house in a small Texas town on the Gulf Coast for a month. When the weather permitted, I walked along a narrow paved road that separated the homes from the Gulf. A few gnarled old trees curved away from the elements that had forced their direction — away from the winds and high water. I began to see the trees the same

1

as I saw people; each, having made an adjustment to time, having a special character and charm.

All the houses had made their own adjustments as well, but I admired one more than any of the others. Each day I'd sit on the pier, look at that house and wonder about who lived there.

One gloomy December morning I followed an impulsive urge and walked up the driveway to meet the owner. I was afraid and nervous until a tiny lady opened a screened door, invited me inside, introduced herself as Anna and spoke as though she had been expecting me. She asked me to please turn off the burner on her cooking stove, share her oatmeal and read to her if I could spare the time.

With only a nod from me, she put several spoons full of sugar and poured heavy cream onto two large bowls of oatmeal. She told me she was a writer and a teacher and led me into her reading room. Several *Godey's Lady's Books* from the 1800s, as well as current fashion and news magazines were on a table in one corner. Five hats, perched on antique wire forms were displayed on a shelf over a daybed. She motioned to me to sit near a large window overlooking the Gulf.

I wanted to know where she had taught school and if she had been published. Anna quickly retorted, "Now, my dear, I did not say I taught school. I said, 'I'm a teacher.' I did not say I'd been published. I said, 'I'm a writer.' If you want to be something, start by saying you are it. You can be a writer, a teacher or a painter. If anyone wants to see your work, show it to them. They can decide if they think you're good at it. I didn't say I'm a good writer. I said, 'I'm a writer.' "

She began telling me about her life. Born in 1892, she started public school in Austin, Texas, in the seventh grade. She'd learned to read when she was four years old; her mother had taught her, using the classics as textbooks. She had gone to the University of Texas from 1912 until 1916. Anna had wanted to study journalism but in those days, it didn't have a journalism department. So she studied literature instead and said she had never regretted it.

"My eyesight deteriorated normally until I turned 80 then it changed rapidly for the worse. I'm practically blind from old age. I only see outlines. I use this magnifying glass with its light to make out words. Working at reading takes away the pleasure, so I don't do much of it anymore. And that's a shame, I've always enjoyed it so — I've enjoyed reading and I've enjoyed reading to others during most of my life. Now my greatest pleasure is having someone read to me. I've made a not quite complete circle, wouldn't you say?

"Tell me about yourself, my dear. I've not been much of a hostess; I've talked too much about myself. Are you here for a special time, Miss Zoe?"

I told her about myself and the vacations I'd enjoyed in her city since I was a child. She reacted to every word I said. Her interest was refreshing. I talked on without feeling rushed.

"My being here today seems to have begun when I was about seven years old. My mother and I were in one of our hair-cutting wars. I wanted bangs and my mother disagreed. I recall saying, 'When I own my own hair, I'll have bangs!'

"Since that day, there's been a never-ending list of questions about who's in charge of me, my heart and my time, and the questions have multiplied. I've been single for two years after an 18 year marriage, and I'm adjusting to that.

"The questions I'm asking now have to do with the reasoning ability of my heart. I'm not trusting the magic of romance as I once did. I'm no longer willing to leave romance to chance or go in any direction where illusion may lead me. Yet I refuse to turn my back on the subject and pretend that romance doesn't matter or doesn't exist. I want to quit running to or from love. I'm ready to take a good look at my friend or my enemy, whoever it turns out to be."

Anna's eyes didn't move from my face. She listened with a rare unhurried silence that made my words become more important to me.

"I'm talking less and asking others fewer questions but I'm thinking and writing more," I continued.

"I'm to be here until the twenty-third of December. Yes, it's a very special time, a time to fix my own hair and the incompatible head and heart beneath it, I hope." Then my voice stopped.

Minutes began to slow down and touch when I looked through the windows that were partially open. The view of the Gulf, the immaculate yard with the trees that curled over and gently touched the roof, the soft breeze blowing the thin white curtains, the smell and taste of the hot oatmeal and Anna's soothing voice created an atmosphere that I knew I would remember for the rest of my life.

"Continue what you're doing. Your time will be well spent here."

Anna was smiling when she asked, "And what did your mother do when you let her know what you wanted?"

"We were looking in a mirror. She stared directly into my eyes, and without a word she gave me the scissors, the comb and the brush. I don't recall another discussion about the subject of my hair ever again."

"That's great!" Anna said. "Now, tell me how you plan to find what you're seeking."

"I've been writing about my feelings since I got my first Big Chief tablet," I told Anna. "I brought enough to reread what I've written over the years to find what all my past owners have had in common. I meditate every day and I continue to write every day. I trust art therapy so I brought clay for play. I have an open plan, and I guess that's my plan — to remain open."

"We'll see!" Anna remarked. After considerable hesitation she said, "Now listen carefully to what I have to say . . .

Letting Go

"If you're trying to change or accept anything about your life, the best place to start is to learn the art of letting go. You'll need the skill every day of your life; so learn and practice, practice and learn.

"Learning how to let go is the beginning of knowledge. Wisdom is found in the actual act of letting go. If you argue with that statement, think back to all the times you tried to let go and failed. Each time you failed, you learned something. When you finally made it, you were wiser, weren't you?

"I like William Cowper's words, *'Knowledge and wisdom far from being one, have oft times no connection. Knowledge dwells in heads replete with thoughts of other men; wisdom in minds attentive to their own. Knowledge is proud that he has learned so much; wisdom is humble that he knows no more.'* "Anna sighed and repeated, " *'. . . Wisdom is humble that he knows no more.'*

"I call it the act of letting go or the art of letting go. You can know everything that is known about letting go, but until you do something — until you act on your knowledge — it's useless. Acting is an art, isn't it? Knowledge is learning how to let go; wisdom comes after you've done it."

Anna's Notebook

She pointed to a large three-ring binder on a table near me and said, "That notebook contains my life." Her notebook, a minimum of three inches thick, bulged with notes, letters to Anna and copies of Anna's letters to her friends and students.

"You won't find a lot of months and years at the top of the pages. I think lessons are dateless. The only thing you need to know about my notebook is that it's a collection of my friends, my students and a few theories that are meaningful to me. I use it for living a loving life."

While she directed, I carefully turned to a worn, paper tab with bold hand printed lettering entitled: "Letting Go." I found the letter Anna wanted to hear. She sat slightly forward and waited for me to begin.

Letter To Virginia

Dear Virginia,

To let go of someone we love has to be one of the most difficult things we do.

Yesterday you and I talked about your dear Cy and how much you want to help him. You said you were aware that both of you need some time and space separate from each other. You then decided how much time he needs, where he needs to spend it and with whom. You asked me if I'd been where you are.

Yes, precious, I've been there many times. Out of my fear, need or greed, I've done exactly what you are doing. Like you, I usually have to be pushed out or have it become so painful that I have no other choice — then I let go.

I'm often reminded of how a Gulf Coast Blue Crab grows. When it outgrows its present shell, it has to shed the old shell and grow a new one. It has to let go completely, hold on to absolutely nothing — all the way to its tiny fingers and claws. It has to let go of the struggle itself.

But can you imagine? To have a choice in this situation? I'm afraid I would want to hold on to the old shell until the end, wouldn't you? Just think of yourself, knowing that to live, you would have to let go of your protection — but also knowing that to stay in the old shell would limit you and eventually kill you.

Growth for the crab is very difficult. It has to risk shedding its old familiar shell — become a soft-shelled crab — and be vulnerable. To survive, it has to go to the bottom, go into the mud and be associated with other crabs also at the bottom.

The surviving crab must have faith that its shell will become firmer and larger each hour. It develops a faith in its pain and learns to believe that it is being prepared for what is currently unknown to it.

Virginia, I know how difficult it is for you to let go of Cy. For me, letting go is an on-going process. I don't know why it's so difficult to let go until I begin holding on to something or someone again. I not only hold on to people, places and things, I hold on to beliefs — beliefs that worked for years but are no longer useful.

The crab story helps me understand that for the rest of my life I will be growing. And like it or not, there will be pain.

What surprises me now is that I can sometimes let go and experience the feelings with gratitude. When I remember why the pain is necessary, I get excited about what's in the future for me. Sometimes I can't wait to shed the shell, learn what I need to learn and get the old shell behind me.

I hope you can relate this to your need to cling to Cy. When he's trying to shed his shell, he's also trying to grow. If you don't let go, you may find yourself clinging to an empty shell. When we cling to someone else, we slow them down and ourselves as well.

To let go of Cy, Virginia, you must have no suggestions for him whatsoever: no arguments, no "if you would only . . . ," no "someday you will . . . ," no, nothing! You have no advice for him . . . nothing more to teach him. You must accept him, just as he is, and relax like the crab. Any struggle, any "buts" and "shoulds" or "ought to's," any "anything," will keep you both where you are now. You have no solution for anyone at this moment in time.

Remember, Virginia, down to the ends of your fingers and claws, you must release any thoughts of holding on. Think of letting go, of letting go! You may let go just so much, feel jealousy and a fear of the unknown and want to cling more than ever before.

When you let go or get kicked off and go through the pain, you'll begin growing your bright clean new beautiful larger shell. So will Cy. This time you'll both be free — free to swim where either of you choose. You will have a shell large enough to grow within. You'll be so large and beautiful that others will ask you how you got that way.

An important thing to think about, just to keep you humble, is that you will one day outgrow this beautiful new shell. Then you will have to go through the pain again. Each time it will be easier though, I promise.

Love,
Anna

I asked Anna what Virginia had learned from this letter, and she answered with a question, "What did you learn, my dear?"

"It's full of messages for me," I laughed. "But on the brighter side, I saw crabs swimming, conversing, having fun, even clinging to each other and others clinging to them."

". . . All the way to the crab trap. Have you ever thought about how much easier it is to let go than it is to kick someone off who is clinging? What happened to Virginia, you want to know? We're all Virginia. Have *you* learned how to let go?" Anna was answering and asking questions nonstop.

"However, there is a time to hold on. My mother told me of a little girl and her father who were out for a morning walk. They were approaching a bridge, and he told her to hold his hand. She refused his hand and said, 'No, Daddy, you hold mine. I may forget and let go of your hand, but I know you would never forget.'

"Use moderation in all things, especially my lessons," she advised.

"Most of us change when the fear of what we don't know is not as frightening as the fear of what we know. How does that statement fit into your search today, Miss Zoe? Are you uncomfortable enough to change? Or do you want someone to keep holding your hand?" Before I had time to think about her questions, she said, "Don't answer — let's do something. You'll have plenty of time to answer those questions."

Anna's Garden

Anna wanted to plant bulbs and to share a "Tall Boy Beer" with me. Well, I'm not a beer drinker and certainly not a warm beer drinker. Nevertheless, we took the beer, two huge sun hats and sat on the curb of her driveway.

"You wouldn't be here if you had learned how to let go. Learn the questions, learn what you want and learn to ask for what's in your control. If you're asking for answers for someone else, you haven't learned the art of letting go.

"And be teachable. Most important, be teachable. Now that's an artist — someone teachable," she said.

"My favorite lesson about being wide open for new learning came from my six-year-old friend, Jessica. She'd received an *F* on a paper. She was quite proud of her work and showed it to me. When her mother told her an *F* was not a good grade, Jessica said, 'Of course it's not a good grade. If I'd made an *A,* I wouldn't have to go to school. I didn't put that *F* on my paper, Mother.'

"Each time we want to learn something new we must become a child again and expect an *F.* Merely opening the mind is nothing. The object of opening the mind, like opening the mouth, is to shut it again with something in it."

Anna wanted to know one specific thing I had learned about myself since the divorce.

"One specific thing? Well, each time I looked at my

appointment book, a portion of my day would be taken with commitments I'd made when I couldn't think of a way to say no to someone. I was charging future time just like I had unlimited credit. I'd got into some passive behavior during marriage, which didn't stop with divorce. My husband had been so good about saying no that he began to sound like a foghorn to me. I can still hear him saying, 'nooooooo' before I ended a question. When *I* couldn't say no, I knew I could depend on him.

"I'm not sure I've learned the lesson very well, but charging future time has been an ongoing struggle. There must be a delicate balance between planning ahead and having free time to enjoy the spontaneous now of future moments. I'm in need of more 'letting go' lessons before I master it, I fear."

"I too have one more crab shell to shed before I become head of that department," Anna remarked. "But, you're welcome to what I've learned," she said without an explanation.

The sun hats on this cloudy December day were the only things around here that didn't make sense. When I asked about the hats, she said, "Let's just 'play like' the sun is out. Don't you have a real question? You're much too quiet, my dear. Speak up anytime. You'll find me not shy at all. I just might talk too much. My hearing is still very good, don't you think?" She smiled, tilting her head to one side with an ear slightly forward.

After reassuring her that her hearing was great, I said, "I always have questions about letting go. I've found it very painful to leave my friends and family, and it's been necessary to leave them at times so we could all grow."

She beamed, "I know what that's all about. I have a story for you."

Swimming Ahead

She and Mava were swimming across a canal, she began telling me, one they had swum many times in the past. This time, however, halfway across the canal, Anna saw the panic in her friend's eyes. Her friend shouted, "I can't swim another stroke."

Anna knew not to go near her, so she swam on ahead, backing up as fast as she could, finally touching bottom, a toe, then a foot — telling her friend how close they both were to safety.

Mava kept paddling and fighting the water until she, too, could touch a toe, then a foot and safety.

Excited and laughing, Anna remembered the scene well. "We were the happiest sight you could ever have seen. We must have looked funny, hugging and carrying on — walking out of that canal with mud to the knees.

"I've remembered that experience each time I've had to swim on ahead. I take that chance almost every day. I think life must be a mini letting-go series . . ."

"Speaking of letting go, Anna," I interrupted, "I'm enjoying this time with you so much you'll have to tell me when to leave. I want everything you're willing to teach me."

"My dear, I am an old lady and I don't get many visitors. They're in such a hurry and have so little time to visit but all I have is time. I've heard that 'A wise man is never less alone than when he is alone.' Now I'm not all that wise, and although I do indeed need my time alone, this is not one of those times. I'll tell you when to go," she promised.

Anna would ask questions, give answers to her own questions, and then change subjects. Yet she kept looping back to the main topic.

"I *like* to get into the subject of letting go. It would be difficult to have lived 90 years without that wisdom. I'll be planting bulbs tomorrow, and you're welcome to study with me.

"Think of everything you need to let go of, and we'll begin our lessons promptly at dawn. The best time to do mental chores is in the morning. Do the physical chores later in the day. You need your mind for the mental things, so catch it when it's fresh. And by all means, give attention to your thoughts. Find out what makes them strong and what causes them to turn inward and attack you."

Listening to her talk and being with her energy all day, I'd forgotten how tiny she was until we hugged good-bye.

"Just a minute, my dear, one more thing you need to know. We won't be working on weekends, but you'll have homework each day. Tomorrow I'd like you to bring a sample of your writing. Choose one that tells me about you and don't prevaricate and don't exaggerate. Today will make more sense tomorrow," she said evasively.

I told her I'd cook breakfast and be responsible for lunch the next day, and she concluded, "I thought you weren't charging future time! Let's take it as it comes."

She smiled and wished me a dream that had within it a dream, and within that dream, a solution and a new question. She turned away from me and walked inside her house.

End of First Day with Anna

Looking at the Gulf as I walked home I tried to imagine what "my crab" looked like. Then I looked at the roofs on some of the homes and smiled at my own analogy. Maybe I could stay in denial and get by with one more roof repair on my crab shell before it caved in.

My thoughts returned to something Anna had said during the day. "I respect the deep yearning inside you. I advise you to value it as truth. Your questions about romance are not a selfish luxury traveling in forbidden territory."

That afternoon, my typewriter took directions without fighting back for the first time in weeks. Thoughts flowed and I wanted to do everything at one time. I searched for a sample of my writing, but I wasn't sure how much I wanted to expose about myself.

"Don't prevaricate about something you do well. If you do it well, say so. And don't spoil it by exaggerating," her words kept repeating themselves in my mind as I searched for the perfect sample. Then I found it. Surely there would be no prevarication and no exaggeration about myself in a letter I'd written to a man I'd never met. I chose *A Letter To Jerry.*

CHAPTER
T W O

Thursday, December 9, 1982

When Anna wanted new thoughts or beliefs, she shouted the thoughts quite loud several times, repeating them softer and softer until they became a whisper, then she said them only to herself. I practiced, "Let go — be teachable," while I walked the mile to Anna's house.

She was ready for me with bananas, heavy cream and a piping hot cup of coffee. Anna wanted to carry her own tray to the reading room. Her voice reflected her enthusiasm, "I can't wait for you to eat! I want to hear what you selected about you. To me it's like opening a new book. The more you know in the beginning, the more interest you have. Of course, that puts more pressure on the writer of the book to keep it going at that momentum. I'll hush up and listen. Let me know when you're ready."

I settled back in my chair. "You asked for something I've written that tells you about me and I think I have found it. Is background to this letter permissible or does each writing have to stand on its own?"

Anna touched my arm and said, "I want to know about you, what you are willing to tell me. If background to one of

13

your writings is important to you, then you can be sure it's important to me."

So I explained, "A girlfriend wanted me to meet a recently divorced friend of hers. She didn't know I'd just begun a hiatus from romantic relationships and that I was reluctant to meet anyone. I invited him to attend a lecture with me and wrote the following letter to Peggy's friend, Jerry, before we met."

Letter To Jerry

Dear Jerry,

Peggy wants us to meet. During our telephone conversation yesterday, we decided to hear a lecture this evening, have dinner and compare where we are in our lives to what we heard at the lecture.

We briefly discussed some of the work we've done on ourselves before and since our divorces. Our talk inspired me to write a few things I'd like you to know about me.

I've learned that I'm not ready for a synergistic relationship. I'm still too dependent for that to be possible. Since a synergistic one is the only kind I'll settle for, I guess I'll have to become what I want from another person.

A big part of me still wants to attach to a special someone and let him take care of all my needs. I would like to have it happen naturally, without effort on my part at all. I would love for him to complete me. My reality is that I'm too close to what I want, to be able to go back but I'm not far enough away from what I don't want to be comfortable.

I'm writing a book. It's like a big bowl of spaghetti. Who knows where it will all end? It just keeps happening. I choose to call it *Santa Claus, God and Love*. I know that the book cannot be until I've worked through the Love part. I've made my peace with Santa and God, but not Love.

I was born on Christmas day. Some of my first memories were of my family and friends telling me about Santa. I loved the magic of Christmas and Santa, and I believed I would get everything I wanted at Christmas time. Although something was always missing, I would hope, "Maybe next year." I went through many years of my life believing in future magic and the magic of another person's power before I abandoned the whole idea.

Slowly I've discovered the Santa I love today. I've learned to expect nothing except what I'm capable of receiving. My Santa is all about the magic of giving and receiving. I can't separate one from the other now. The ultimate gift to me is to have been given something to give; something that someone wants.

". . . Rings and things are excuses for gifts, the only true gift is a portion of one's self." Ralph Waldo Emerson's words help me to keep in perspective what I believe about my Santa.

The next thing I remember being in conflict about was God . . . I was taught, or I decided to believe, that all I had to do was pray about any crisis and everything would be perfect again.

I believed what I had been taught until I had a crisis. My mother was in a car accident. I prayed during the drive to the scene of the accident, so I believed that everything would be all right. When we arrived there, she was dead! My 15-year-old mind decided to discard the word God from my vocabulary but never to tell anyone about my decision.

Needless to say, the decision to discount everyone who mentioned God proved to be as immature as thinking that all I had to do was pray about a crisis.

It's taken many years of pain to force me into what I believe about God. I now have a quite unshakable belief in God as I understand the word. And I can accept what you believe without a need to change you or me.

Today I'm having a problem with the word Love.

The movies, my friends, sisters, my parents — all said it would be one thing or another. I've tried to plug their interpretation of the word Love into all my romantic relationships, and all I've learned is that I don't know what I believe. I'm afraid that Love does not exist as I programmed it, and the search scares me. But so did the search for my Santa and my God.

My Santa and my God keep me going. They keep me searching. They keep me asking questions. They keep me confronting my emotional pain with faith, hope and education. They keep me knowing that if I will experience these feelings, if I continue to ask and to receive and believe, then I, too, may find Love as I understand it.

What if it's not out there at all?

What if it's not in another person?

What if Love is only a projection of all my experiences with the word? What if?

As I write I'm aware of how great it feels to feel 'that' feeling.
Who wants to give up all that?

Well, Jerry, now that you know what I don't know and that I
accept you just as you are, that I welcome you and I will continue
to welcome you along this journey, that I don't need you but I do
want you in this life, that you are free to be you as you allow me
to be free to be what I'm becoming, do you still want to hear John
Bradshaw speak?

Sincerely,

Zoe

"Did Jerry go to the lecture with you?"

"Yes, and when he read the letter, he told me I didn't have
to become so independent to have a relationship like the
one I wanted. That may very well have been true, but as I
explained to him, I had decided that I have to find what I
believe. We attend lectures together and share our secrets
like two little kids just discovering boys and girls. This time
the discovered kids are ourselves."

Anna, smiling and applauding, said, "My praise is for your
courage! Someone with insight, someone without pretense,
someone not willing to jump into another marriage before
being separate from the last. I knew I'd live to meet another
one."

She settled down and began, "So you think you're
divorced. That's what the judge said. I think you're
divorcing. I don't care how long the papers have been
signed. If you're holding on, if you aren't at peace, you are
not separate. You are no different from the 'you' who was
married or the 'you' who was single before you were
married, but you don't know that yet.

A Lone Being Living Alone

"We're all alone. We were separated at birth and we will
be separate when we die. You are a lone being, and you are
now living alone. No one, not your husband, your child,
your friend or that illusive one-and-only can guarantee you
they'll be with you for the remainder of your life. Nor can
you guarantee that you will be with any one until he or she

dies. I want you to grieve in that awareness," she demanded. Anna repeated, "We are all alone."

I screamed at that truth, "I don't want to be alone! I don't want to be separate!" She was speaking directly to a void within me that nothing had filled, in or out of marriage. I didn't want to hear what she was saying.

Blunt and eloquent, Anna now admitted, "The impact of that awareness for myself caused two reactions in me. First, I felt dead and hopeless, and second, I felt a personal power and responsibility I'd not experienced until that moment of acceptance. I accepted that I'm all there will ever be of me. Any changes, additions or subtractions were also up to me."

Peek-A-Boo

She walked behind a door and started playing Peek-a-boo. I knew a lesson was coming, so I played the game and waited.

"Most of us didn't have anyone to explain the meaning of this game," Anna said. "I'm here, but you can't see me. We have to learn to believe that a loved one is here or there when we can't see or touch them. We can be together and apart at the same time. That's all I want to say about peek-a-boo for now. Remember what I just said and tell me about synergism," she persisted.

I tried to explain, "I think of two people who have completed their personal development so that they have the emotional maturity to enjoy a truly adult relationship and, and, uh, uhh, know all about 'peek-a-boo!' Anything more said begins to sound like fantasy, doesn't it?" I stumbled to a verbal halt and watched Anna walk away.

Grow Where You Are Planted

"It's playtime," Anna announced as she gathered a few bulbs from different cartons and put them into a paper sack. "Let's plant some bulbs and talk."

She took several bulbs and threw them. Anna instructed, "Dig the holes precisely where the bulbs fall. The tulips will look far more natural, and you can learn a most valuable lesson from the experience. Grow where you are planted! Life has a way of hurling us in all directions. Some of us grow and bloom, while others complain and die. When I'm ready to die, I'll quit planting bulbs. Until then, I'll have something to look forward to in the springtime."

Anna continued to throw bulbs and talked about creativity. "I believe in creation, creativity and a creator. I may very well be all three. I plant something just about every day, and I always get more back than I put in. It's like Mother Nature and I are playing games with each other.

"Use a sharp kitchen knife. It cuts the grass roots faster than anything I've found and is just the right size. Take one scoop of dirt out with a large kitchen spoon, place the bulb in the hole and then *let go!*

"You wouldn't think of pulling one of them up to check its roots to see if it's growing, would you? So, accept yourself as you are . . . and, if we look for the perfect spot to put our little bulbs, we may never get planted." Laughing, talking and digging holes at the same time, she bumped me away from the last bulb to be planted that day.

We quit working early in the afternoon. My assignment for the next day from Anna was to bring what I'd written on relationships.

"Be here about the same time tomorrow morning, and please make me a copy of your letter to Jerry for my notebook." She also wanted a folder entitled "Santa."

End of Second Day with Anna

I worked until midnight. All I'd accomplished was reading over and over what I'd written about relationships. My concern was that it would be shallow and trivial compared to Anna's erudition. She'd cautioned me against "absolutizing and cementing theories" without personal experiences enough to be versatile. "If they have value, you'll find they cross with other theories. There's nothing new. Remember, all our great ideas were stolen from us by earlier writers," she'd said several times.

I decided I'd hear tomorrow what I needed to learn tomorrow and I went to sleep.

CHAPTER

THREE

Friday, December 10, 1982

When I walked into the kitchen, Anna's first words were, "This day will be one to remember! After breakfast, I'd like you to read my letter to Rachael. I get so excited about being your teacher. There aren't enough hours in the day to give you what I want you to know. All I ask is that you pass these lessons on, and pass them on to those who will be passing them on.

"Let me warn you. People will play the same games with you as Mother Nature plays with the bulbs: the more you give, the more you'll get back. Don't expect to get even. You never will!"

During breakfast, we chatted about my evenings alone and what I did with that time. Anna had an interest in everything I did, especially my clay work.

"You know by now that I can talk on and on and waste as much time as anyone, don't you? You also know that when I have a plan, I stick to my plan."

She gave me a folder with today's lesson inside. I followed her into the reading room where there was a light fragrance of sandalwood incense smoldering in an old brass container she'd placed on the coffee table. Anna told me the incense was to prevent any atmosphere burn-out I may be developing. She curled up in her chair and waited for me to read.

A Letter To Rachael

Dear Rachael,

My, oh my, how I laugh, just thinking about the first time I saw you after a long absence. I thought Atlas had shrugged and you had caught the whole thing; you, a beautiful, 40-year-old woman with the weight of the world on your shoulders.

You said, "Anna, I'm divorced after four years of marriage and I think there's something wrong with me. So I'm back for all the old and new lessons.

"My friends tell me I have to have somebody to be happy. I love my life," you kept saying, "I'm not obsessed with anyone, and I don't want to spend all my energy looking for that someone. I'm not concerned about having someone in sickness and in health. I'm taking care of my sickness and my health just fine. When I'm sick, I let those who care for everyone else care for me — doctors and nurses. I'm insured. I don't fear sickness. What are they talking about?" you asked with such seriousness.

"I want to have my own life, Anna." You kept right on making sense. I couldn't stop you and I didn't want to. I was hoping you were hearing yourself. When you finally wound down, I told you that my generation and those before me have passed this way of thinking on to you and your friends. You see, Rachael, in my day that is how it was. Togetherness was all we knew.

We all sacrificed for each other. Women weren't the only ones who gave up their interests, hobbies and dreams for the family. Our men were just as frustrated as we. They had sacrificed their youthful dreams to feed, clothe and shelter the babies who were coming much too fast. You inherited our frustrations and the ways we found to deal with our dependency on each other. You are the beneficiary of that togetherness and closeness, including our fibs about how wonderful it was.

Together and close. The way most of our ancestors thought of it was being locked in with no breathing room for individuation. That's how I see those marriages now.

Scrambled Eggs

It seems from here that the healthiest members of those families were the ones who went for help. We couldn't live in that kind of scrambled-egg environment where everyone thought alike, felt alike and experienced reality in the same way.

When we began to see things as we saw them, felt what we were feeling and thought what we were thinking — we were told that we were crazy. We went for help for our crazy selves and learned that all the scrambled eggs need separate yolks. We all need our own boundaries.

Some of us found our own boundaries, some of us went back to the system and later broke out and some folks never left home. If I've confused you, let me say that couples come together to get certain needs met. If we are in a healthy environment and we get those needs met, we're free to get other needs met, too. Needs change and if the environment is flexible enough, so do the people in it.

Egg Yolks

I like to use eggs to explain this more simply. The yolk represents the center of ourselves — what we think, hear, see and value, the part that grows. A clearly defined yolk has clearly defined beliefs, convictions, opinions and principles, yet it is always open for new information. The size of our yolk determines the people we are attracted to and those attracted to us. If we are growing, the yolk gets larger and that's why our world keeps changing. If the people we're around aren't growing, we move on. And we do that through a painful letting-go process.

Watch the family of a recovering alcoholic. The alcoholic cannot stay sober unless he or she is growing. If the spouse is not growing, you can be sure divorce is right around the corner. The same thing happens if the non-alcoholic gets help. When we grow, people around us either grow, get left, die or scramble with another.

Egg Whites

Think of the white of the egg as emotions that we all have. If our emotions were accepted as normal when we were very young, they don't dominate our lives today. We were fortunate if we had someone who understood our emotions and walked through the rough times with us. If no one was there for us when we were anxious or afraid, we felt overwhelmed.

What happens when we are anxious or afraid today? The same thing. Our yolk is immediately overpowered by our emotions, and we can't think. The white of the egg can cloud our yolk and dominate us. The smaller the yolk, the more we can be overpowered.

Our emotions, or the white of the egg — the sticky stuff that attaches to other people — is determined by the size of our yolk. The white of the egg decreases as the yolk increases.

The hope is that we don't have to be a victim to our emotions. We can find some ways to increase the size of our yolk if we are willing to go through some emotional pain and claim some uncomfortable truths about ourselves.

Remember, Rachael, the people we attract have the same need to attach as we have. That their yolk is the same size as ours is only one more reason we can't find what is missing in us in another person. Sandwich that in your memory, Rachael.

Staying Separate Together

To get out and stay out of an unhealthy scrambled egg family is nearly impossible. Everyone in the scrambled egg is screaming, "Come back or else!" If we do get out, we find our yolk is so tiny that most of us attach to the nearest body, and we start another scrambled egg and pass it on to the next generation. I think that's why we have so much emotional discomfort today. Adult children of alcoholics have just begun to recognize a need to stop all this insanity. It's multigenerational, my dear. All this togetherness didn't start with you or me.

Today the pendulum seems to be swinging toward living alone. I watch what you people are doing — you are physically running alone. Running with people, yes, but you are in competition with yourselves. Some of you are taking responsibility for your own lives. If there's a special person in your life, it's a someone who allows you to be what you are, separate from each other — not scrambled.

When our yolk is clearly defined, we can run separate or with someone, just like the joggers do. We can be in competition with ourselves. We can have our own thoughts. We can see what *we* see while we run through life, and we can hear what tapes *we* want to hear along the way. We can run or not run. We have a choice if we are separate. Scrambled eggs can't do that. If the boss runs, everybody runs.

The scrambled-egg tradition dictates that we take the blame for all the unhappiness around us. And in turn, we can blame everyone other than ourselves for *our* unhappiness. If we have our own yolk, we know who is responsible for our happiness.

Sorting For Happiness

Ah, happiness! That illusive, magical, sought-after feeling that we all want. It's everywhere, I believe. We can find happiness by changing that magnificent mind of ours, and we can change our mind anytime. I find it in a bulb being planted or when the storms come off the Gulf or anywhere I choose to look.

I recall being at a funeral. The person being buried was my youngest sister. Butterflies were everywhere that time of the year. My little sister had loved butterflies. She knew everything about them. She philosophized about them.

She said many times, "Butterflies are here for a short time, but they seem to have time enough."

I enjoy this fresh new way of looking at her philosophy. I found something special at her funeral, but I certainly had to look for it. So I've learned to look for happiness. And I find it everywhere. I believe this moment with you is all there is — right now, this second, Rachael. I'm enjoying it so much. My heart is full. I'm happy. When I write to you or talk about you, I'm with you.

I don't have anyone sitting here telling me how to enjoy my time with you. No one taught me to look for happiness. This is what I believe. So this, my dear, is my reality.

If you are one of those who doesn't sort for happiness, you won't find it very often. Teach yourself to look for the highs. They can become instant gratification.

When I plant a bulb, I'm aware of the wonders of this world. What has to happen so that this bulb can change into a beautiful tulip? It's magic! Biologists teach me about the transition but then join in my wonderment; emerging from the dark ground, looking for the sunshine, finding it and willing to be what it is, a tulip.

There it is — I planted it — for all to see. That's a gift. A gift to me and a gift from me to all who will take time to see it. It's up to me. This very second! I remind myself to look for happiness.

Happiness Abuse

I told a teenaged drug abuser what drugs were going to do to him, and he couldn't hear me. He had no reference into the future for what I was saying. All he knew was what pleasure he had experienced in the past using the drugs.

When I began asking, "What are the drugs doing for you?" we could hear each other. He told me. I listened. I could then help him sort for ways to accomplish the same feeling or purpose without the drugs. I'm a lot like him. I love my highs — my natural highs. I sometimes think that I abuse happiness, I find so much of it.

Rachael, I'm happy for you. We must talk about your new life and new way of thinking more.

Love,
Anna

When I finished the letter, I put it back into the folder and placed it on the table. I was thinking about all the studying and the many lectures I'd attended on family systems and how she had summed it all up in an egg.

Anna said, "You remind me of Rachael. Your search is the same, isn't it? What do you think?"

With both arms outstretched, inviting her in for my biggest hug, I let her know. "That's a happy letter. A few minutes ago, I wanted to rush out and begin looking for happiness. The message, I reminded myself, is to look for it this second! I'd love to read it over and over, that's what I think.

"Your wonderful egg hypothesis reminds me of a wife who was trying not to react negatively to her grumpy husband's request for one egg scrambled and one egg fried. 'You ate only one of your eggs,' she cheerfully observed, then asked, 'Is something wrong with the other?' Determined not to give up his bad mood, he said, 'You scrambled the wrong egg.' "

I told Anna that I'd scrambled the wrong egg so many times during marriage that after reading her letter, it was exciting to think that maybe I came into the world scrambled.

"My lesson plan for you is full of 'egg yolk boundary builders,' " she laughed. "The boundaries are porous — they allow for plenty of input and output. When your yolk is large enough, your head and heart won't be scrambled, I promise. You can have what you want.

"You can't not find what you want — if you know what you want. If what you want is possible in the world, it's possible for you — if you believe that it's possible for you."

Birth Or Death

Anna, no longer smiling, began.

"We've talked about the importance of letting go and about having a choice about happiness. We simply must not turn that page without taking a bold look at death. When I'm faced with a death I think is impossible for me to handle or adjust to, I say to myself, 'My wisdom is a meditation of life.' That saying reminds me that I did not die and that death is part of living. I'm not recommending the saying; I'm telling you that's what I say.

"My husband discussed death freely," Anna said. "For instance, his 11-year-old niece asked him what became of her mother when she died. In his gentle way he said, 'If a fetus could talk, it would say, "I want to stay in this warm place — I can't possibly live outside here. I couldn't breathe; this fluid is my life. I'm connected to my mother — I'm totally dependent on her. There's no way I can survive outside here. No thanks!'

" 'One day a force greater than itself forces it out; and lo and behold, it's breathing and crying. It is alive!

" 'Another day comes in the life of each of us, when we are forced into another dimension — one we don't know about. This is called Death — Death of this life.

" 'Your question about your mother is the beginning of a philosophy that you'll be updating until the very moment that you are forced out of this life.' "

A Meditation Of Life

"That's worth remembering," Anna said, "but, what happens to that last breath? No one has caught it and analyzed it. It just hits the ceiling, I guess. I haven't concentrated on my death as much as I've concentrated on ways to let go of my loved ones who have died or my loved ones who are living-dead.

"Giving up a belief or a loved one — is that a birth or a death? That's why I say, 'My wisdom is a meditation of life.' I decided at a young age to concentrate on living, and I've never been sorry about that decision."

Anna gave me the folder and said, "Read what I wrote to Susan and we'll talk more about letting go of our loved ones."

Another undated letter began:

A Letter To Susan

Dear Susan,

Thank you for telling me what's happening in your family. Your little Sara, 15 years old, with no desire to live and threatening to kill herself.

How tragic!

When we talked, I could only give you my experience and my hope. I know the fear of "holding on" and the fear of "letting go."

You told me you had contacted a large clinic in your city and that you want to believe that "out there" — "out there" somewhere — there is someone who can pinpoint the exact problem and tell you exactly what to do.

You said you had read my crab story and you want to know how to let her go. You said you are willing to die for her but you have no more life to give anyone.

You've decided that you are clinging to each other, exchanging places — she clings to you until you move away; and when she knows no way to let go except to destroy herself, you begin clinging to her.

You've asked me to relate this to the crab story because you need something very simple.

Well, lovely people, you can cling to what is. Your child is alive right now. There are some of us not so fortunate. For now, cling to the known. All your loved ones are safe at this moment.

Also understand that because we love, we must let go — we stand by, we give help only when we're asked. We can help others by loving them, and we can love them without trying to run their lives. The more we hold on to our loved ones, the more they try to escape.

Make yourself known to other crabs. Talking to others who are where you are will give you hope, acting on the sharing will give you strength, surviving will give you experience and experience will give you wisdom.

Finally, by letting her go, knowing that you have done all you can do, she will be free to sink into the mud, gain her own strength, continue to grow and be her own crab. Or she may die — but not by your hands, not by your clinging onto her.

Do something good for her and for yourself. Show her your strength and teach her the art of letting go, by example. Let her make her own mistakes. We all want to help our loved ones toughen their shells in the open waters, without the growing pains. We can only retard them by doing that.

I pray that you can love each other to safe waters. You're dealing with a big one, Susan. If you hold on to her with your love, she may kill herself. If you let her go with your love, she may kill herself. I Love You, Susan.

I'm here!

Love,
Anna

Is Love Priceless?

She surprised me with her question, "How can we lose anything or anyone we have once loved? We'll have the treasures in our memories. Once we know love, we recognize love. When we give love, we learn about love. If it hurts, ask if love was freely given — not what love costs. Is it priceless or not? If it can be taken from us, we are not 'it,' and when we are not 'it,' we have to let go."

Her statements and questions were making me mighty uncomfortable.

"Anna, was that last mouthful fertilizer or plant food?" I asked her.

"It's all the same, isn't it?" was her quick response. "When you think of it, there is always an ending. We don't plan an ending in the beginning. Who looks at a new pet with death in mind? Or a first date and thinks about the death of the new loveship? I've outlived practically all my relatives and friends, including a son and husband. When I feel sad about my lost ones, I remember and smile at my precious husband's question, 'What if death is Mother Nature playing peek-a-boo?' "

Life After Here

"Anna, what do you believe about life after death?" I asked.

"Life after death? I've been amused at that question more than once in my lifetime. I'll answer you with a question, and I hope I leave you with more questions," she said.

"Who do you admire? Isn't it someone who can take nothing and make it into *something* — a story, a thought, a passing comment. What gives it meaning? Is it the transmitter or the receiver, the seed or the gardener?

"Remember that it's what you do with what I say, not what I say.

"How can any of us be wrong about what we believe about life after here? Each of us is an authority on that subject.

"A friend of mine once asked, 'Is there meaning to all this life, or were we just another accident in the evolution of cells, protoplasm and a bacteria that took the form of life?' "

Anna smiled then asked, "Is there meaning? Who took that *nothing* and made it into *something?* Who is creative? Are the writers and painters the only artists? Are the carpenters not creative? What do the gardener and the fisherman create? And what about all the professionals, scientists, business people and the homemakers? Don't we all take what could be meaningless and make it into *something?* Isn't that creativity and creation — and doesn't that make us all creators?

"To make happiness out of a thought is what I call *something.* The story of Santa tells me that someone took *nothing* and gave it *something* — hope to many little hopeless kids. They took an idea, made a story and gave hope. Is that not *something?* Is God any different? Man looked for all the signs of hope, made a story and gave it meaning — gave us religions. Now isn't that *something?*

"What do I believe? Do I believe in life after here? I certainly do. I believe that life will go on after me and after you. I like to believe that after the sun eats up the earth there will be life — a form of life I don't know about because God keeps that a secret. That secret gives me hope and a challenge.

"I like the idea that God keeps it all a secret.

"In your letter to Jerry you referred to the magic of Christmas and that there is always something missing. Well, I love knowing there is always something missing — something I don't know — something about which no one on this earth can be absolutely certain.

"I like to make up words and add to words, so I call God "Good." When I'm being Good, I'm being God-like. Any Good God would understand, don't you think? I also like to believe that all religions are saying the same thing, 'God is Good.' After all the talk and arguing, the bottom line is that everybody's God is Good for them or they would give it up.

"You have ample opportunity while you're on this earth to do something with nothing, to be creative, to take a thought and add to it. To be Good means that you believe in Good, doesn't it?

"When you think you are nothing, be aware of this unique opportunity to make *something* out of *nothing* — *YOU.* When life is hard, mold it like you do your clay. Make something out of that hardness.

"I'd like to be asked what gives life meaning? Maybe it's all in what's missing at Christmas. For me, it's not what is here on earth — or there after death. It's what I do about what is not here that is important to me. Isn't that a fun idea? I'll have to be forced out of this life because I love it here — in this womb. When I'm forced out of this one, I'm sure that if there is any kind of opportunity to be creative, I'll find it. Have I given you any new questions?"

"Yes, pages of them," I answered and looked at my notes.

Anna and I took a break. We straightened the house as we walked about, throwing things in the wastebasket. She talked the entire time.

The Art Of Discard

"Letting go, choices, death, birth and all our living lessons now bring us to the art of discard."

Anna almost shouted, "Discard! I think one of the biggest problems in life is getting rid of the things we no longer use. From a desk full of papers to a simple thought, in order to enjoy the exhilarating now, we must learn to discard!"

"Come to think of it," Anna said in a calm voice, "Mother Nature is just about the only entity I know of that discards her waste properly. Just think about the fresh flowers and new fruits that vicious little discarder brings us every season.

"Some poet said, 'We rise by stepping on our dead selves.' I've often wondered if my dead self is what I've learned to live without. Is what I've learned and forgotten, not also what I've discarded, including all of what I've 'let go?'

"I have another question," Anna continued. "Is our past or dead self a contribution to what Carl Jung said about the collective unconscious? I 'think' he believed that everything we learn goes into that collection, so it's never lost. We can all draw from that wisdom.

"When I'm being especially creative, I like to think that I've tapped into that source, don't you? The collective unconscious may very well be one of the powers behind prayer and faith. Again, I only have questions but every now and then, I trust my own answers. It's what I learn after I've learned it all that impresses me about this life.

"And another thing, I'm not sure that the past determines the present. Why not let the present determine the past? I can change my past by changing how I remember my past. I simply change how I think about my past by adding whatever was missing. I'll teach you how I reframe all that in a few days," she stated with confidence.

"It's time to stop now. I've not forgotten your relationship work. I thought I could save my listening time until the afternoon, so I could tune you in or out," she teased. "Listening is work, isn't it? Let's start late mid-morning on Monday. I'll have a surprise for us if the weather permits."

End of Third Day with Anna

Walking home, I reviewed the day and her first words that morning, "This day will be one to remember." That it was!

First Weekend

My friend Cindy and her daughters, Kimberly and Jennifer, visited with me and spent the weekend at her parents' vacation home, which was only a few houses away from the one I was renting. Anna and her crab stories impressed Cindy, but the seven year old and nine year old wanted to know why I'd bother to listen to anything that sounded like school during a vacation. Cindy had been very worried about me. For me to leave the city for a month in the winter seemed a bit unusual to most of our friends. However, Cindy's worry turned to humor before she left. She asked, "Should I tell everybody you're in 'Clinging Crab Clinic Training?' "

CHAPTER
FOUR

Monday, December 13, 1982

I saw Anna from a distance, cleaning an old wrought iron table and chairs that sparkled from the many layers of white paint and years of use and care. But then everything sparkled around Anna.

"Picky-Nicky" Luncheon

Her first words were, "Your surprise is having lunch with me outside. We've plenty to do to prepare for the event. My husband would have called this a 'picky-nicky luncheon.' He thought I was much too picky. We need a centerpiece for the table, if you will, my dear. Things must be pretty and show some creativity for me to enjoy them fully. The extra effort makes the birds and squirrels happier, I believe, don't you?"

Preparing lunch had become one more thing I enjoyed with Anna. We made an exceptionally good soup with seafood, chicken broth and fresh vegetables. Anna heated some crusty French rolls and put globs of creamy butter onto them before I had a chance to stop her.

The table was located in back of her home, but we could be seen from the road. Although there were only a few cars, the drivers slowed them to a near stop — two of them turned around and drove by again. We could have been a scene from a movie. The atmosphere was intimate, the conversation stimulating and the actors definitely loved one another. Only a few days before, we were sitting on the curb with beers and sun hats. These pictures will have to remain in my memory. Who would believe me?

I loved the quiet full silence as I looked at the Gulf. In the distance a ship was moving slowly toward the Port of Houston. A few lazy sea gulls dipped in and out of the smooth surfaced water. The water reflected the tranquility I was feeling, not one ounce of turbulence below. This was one of those rare times when I was exactly where I wanted to be, with the perfect person, doing what I wanted to be doing. I was feeling what I loved feeling — at peace and very, very safe.

I looked at the green leaves, dead twigs and moss table arrangement; and I thought of Brent, a creative contemporary flower designer.

Brent does an orchid arrangement that is one of my favorites. He uses a branch from a curly willow tree, an orchid here and there, with a small amount of moss draped over the tiny water holders of the orchids. Oh, well, so what if my quasi-exotic simulation needed more than orchids.

Anna pulled her chair closer and said, "Your weekend was eventful, I hope."

I told her about Cindy, the girls and Cindy's closing remarks. When I mentioned "Clinging Crab Clinic Training," Anna interrupted delightedly.

"Laura, my therapist friend, and I have been looking for a good slang phrase to fit all the 12-step programs, all the different kinds of therapy and all the treatment centers. That's a great one! 'Cling Clinics!' You tell Cindy I'll be using it, beginning now, with your training on relationships."

I began to talk about a group I belong to which is made up of eight women.

"Jealousy, possessiveness, dependency, fear of being alone, boredom, sexual attraction, addiction to excitement and impulsivity are common topics of conversation in our group. And we're not talking about our clients. We initially came together because we weren't getting some of our own needs met. We all work in the psychology profession. With good reason, our friends and families don't understand our needs. Most people can discuss the details of their work — we can't, not even with each other. We often hear people say, 'Don't you know better than to feel certain feelings? Or, how can you help someone else, if you don't have it all together?'

"Their questions remind me of myself when a teacher said, 'I don't know' to a question I'd asked. For several days, I discounted everything she said. If she didn't know all things, how could she know anything, I reasoned. The frustration of our loved ones and friends is no different from our own frustration. We would like to meet the ultimate authority also. Now, we have our group." Anna caught the humor of that remark so I continued lightheartedly.

"We have full access to a range of emotions, and we are free to express them with no fear of getting stuck in any one feeling. We use the group to work on our romantic partner problems, and you'll have no problem imagining the numerous theories we've discussed and the frustrations we feel when knowledge fails us and our romantic bonds don't bind.

"We've found that it's easy to feel and act independent when all our needs are being met. However, when finances aren't there, when out of the ordinary change of any kind takes place or when we experience jealousy, fear or anxiety, we revert back to basic survival tactics and cling to a romantic partner with the same primitive jungle survival grasping as any animal seeking food, water and shelter. One member said she feels like a lost ant in a rain storm looking for a little piece of bark to climb onto when she is in a crisis."

A gust of wind forced the flowerless arrangement off the table. The metal container fell with a thud. Before I could get out of my chair, Anna said, "Let's worry about that mess another time. I want to know what you need to hear yourself say next."

"The value of this group for me has been living proof that intelligence has very little to do with emotional maturity. I've learned that accumulating knowledge isn't painful. Personal growth is painful!

Triangulation

"I'm sure that it's old knowledge to you, Anna, that a quick fix to escape something stressful at home or at work is to divert attention to a new romantic partner. An affair can take just enough of the tension off the problems in a marriage or a job to make the situation bearable. Affairs are a very common way to avoid being intimate, you know.

"When the pressure of intimacy begins to build, we offset the tension with something. We call that something our 'Triangles.' "

Anna interrupted, "Laura, my therapist friend, lectures to patients in alcoholism treatment centers on 'The Fear of Intimacy.' I should have said she lectures in Cling Clinics. We'll be reading some of her work in a day or two.

"You're right. What better way can you think of to avoid intimacy or getting close than to divert the anxiety to another person? Laura calls it 'Triangulation.' She makes it rhyme with Strangulation. Continue, dear, you have my interest."

I leaned back. "Anna, I want to acknowledge some men I know. They've had to put their emotions on the back burner for so many generations that many of them have come out of this quagmire without their emotions ruling them. They've been accused of having no feelings, of not being in touch with their feelings and of being unable to express their feelings by women like me who are governed by our emotions. The men have something we want, and we have something the men want. I think we've all confused each other. Women have had the luxury for generations of expressing emotions, which some of our men would like to have had. But many of them have accomplished feats they couldn't have if they had allowed their feelings to dominate their every move. I envy those men, and I feel sorry for them at the same time. I enjoy bringing this spicy topic up in the group for discussion over and over.

"And, Anna, you should see each member's shopping lists of requirements for a mate. We get so specific! If he meets all our major requirements, but he is a different height or hair color or less hair maybe, or lived one year too many or too few, or has one degree more or less than our shopping list calls for, do you think we change our criteria? Absolutely not!

"Maybe this is a good time to talk about sex addicts. Surely, you know I'm not saying that all experimental sex will lead to sexual addiction. Sexual addicts say their addiction is the same as an alcoholic's increase in the tolerance to alcohol. More and more sexual experiences are needed to accomplish the same level of excitement and the lists of partners can get plenty weird. I'll bet you've never heard of Sex Anonymous, have you?"

She said, "No, I haven't, but I can get them some new members if they want to start a group here. That's one group I don't think I'll be joining."

I thought about some of the family problems and legal hassles these people have and, I continued, "Just like any addiction, it's incomprehensible if you don't identify. But sexual addiction is one of the many relatives we've inherited from our scrambled-egged ancestors."

I mentioned to Anna the synergistic bond, which is based on other needs and suggested that we discuss it later.

Syn Energy

Anna said, "Just stay right where you are. It's dessert time. I'll create something more energizing than a new romantic bond. In fact, it may be harder to get rid of than a fusion."

She returned with my favorite Sara Lee cheesecake to which she had added walnuts and half a banana. "Let's call this our 'Syn Energy.' There's fresh coffee brewing. Will you remember to get it in a few minutes, please, Lady Zoe?

"You girls are good for each other, aren't you? Sounds to me like all of you need a living philosophy rather than more theories. You're getting to the age where it all begins to come together and you won't be talking about your philosophy. You'll be living it! That's what I call having your own integrity, your own value and your own worth. Your group probably calls it 'locus of control.' Nothing's new!"

Anna continued, "Whatever theory you accept, you must ultimately act yourself into a way of thinking. How can you think yourself into a way of acting? Maybe that's what you meant in your letter to Jerry when you said, 'I'm trying to become what I expect from another person.' Or you said something like that."

She asked, "How can you know who you are until you become who you are?"

"I have no idea, Anna. Aren't you getting tired? I am, and I still have a stack of notes to go over. Can we take a break?" I asked.

That delightful lady reached across the table with her delicate touch and said, "When I tire of you, it will be much like when I quit planting bulbs."

A Jog Walk

Anna wanted to "jog-walk" to my house and have me drive her home later. She knew the history of every home on the beach. Anna described the people who lived there with a total absence of gossip, good or bad. When I met them, I was free of prejudice.

Anna talked about the history of my rented home and the people who'd lived there through the years. We walked around the yard and into the house. It had a large dining room table which was perfect for us to spread out our papers. Anna adjusted to her new environment with ease.

"Where are we with your lesson? Let's not get off track just because teacher let you out to play," Anna disciplined.

"How we get our needs met through our romantic partners, learning to recognize our repeats, our disappointments, the honesty among our group members and what we are learning from each other is where I am," I said.

Chattel Mortgage Bundle

I continued, "What I've observed about our group is that we each seem to have an emotional bundle of *Romantic Love* to give away. We carry this bundle around, loaded with everything we've learned about the word *Love.*

"Our bundles have every belief and saying from every friend, family member, minister and teacher that we've known, including Adam and Eve and all the literature, poetry and mythology we've ever read. We've kept every compliment, those we deserved as well as those we didn't get. It's full of what we expected and didn't expect and what the last person did to us or for us.

"Without bothering to look at what's worth keeping and what needs to be thrown out, we just pick up our 'Chattel Mortgage Bundle' from one man and plop or drop or drag it across a new partner.

"It's easy to understand why we've had so much trouble getting out of miserable situations. If we got out of a miserable situation, we would have to pick up our bundle. And who wants to carry all that 'stuff' around? We certainly don't! It becomes increasingly difficult to find someone to take it all on."

Anna asked me what the other girls were doing about their bundle.

I said, "I don't know, Anna. I don't know if I'm the only one willing to take a look or if I'm the only one who hasn't already looked. I know that I'm afraid and I have faith at the same time. I'm afraid of the empty space I'll have to fill if I have to give up all my old beliefs. Yet I have faith that whatever replaces it, will have to be better than what I've been carrying around. I can't answer your question about the other girls.

"One thing we all agree on is that our relationships are more honest when we discuss our problems with the group. Our goal is not to use our men friends as therapists to us or play therapists to them, and that's difficult for me.

"One member put on a skit for us. She said, 'My emotions are screaming out to get their needs met, so I've decided to give them all the basics. Everything needs nourishment, especially my emotions.' She made an issue about women who continue to put more into a relationship than they are getting in return. She reached to the heavens for help when she said, 'It doesn't rain in the desert because it only rains where it gets something back, so why should I let my emotions dry out from lack of nourishment?' She talked on and on about how she gives her emotions air by talking about them and how she feeds them with all the new feedback she gets from the group. She wrapped her arms around herself dramatically and said, 'I shelter them with the protection and comfort of your experiences, and I love them by accepting them as normal. When they aren't satisfied with all that, I cry, rant, rave, cuss and scream and kick my heels on the floor.' "

Anna said she'd like to be a fly on the wall during one of my group meetings. We ended the lesson without an assignment.

On the drive back to her home, Anna said, "I'll need to sleep on what I've heard from you today. There has to be an easier way. If there is, we'll find it, I promise."

Moon Magic

I had dinner that evening in a restaurant built partially over the water. The waves splashed against a large rock at one corner of the restaurant and the moonlight reflected in the water for miles. A surge of loneliness overwhelmed me. I smiled as I imagined telling my group about the argument I could have made in favor of fusing, avoiding and experimenting with a romantic partner in this atmosphere if I'd had the opportunity. I stuffed my mouth full of baked potato and swallowed my feelings right along with it.

End of Fourth Day with Anna

Alone in my rented bed I began thinking about my quest to learn the meaning to me of the word *Love*. I was no longer frightened about holding on to the bundle a while longer. It was uncomfortable and unfamiliar but not frightening. I was enjoying the free feeling of not being obsessed with someone, and I loved being in total possession of my time. Yet lying there my bundle became increasingly important to me. I began to accept that the bundle was not something I could give away, throw away, grow from or have taken from me. It was an appendage, an emotional pack and mine alone. It was and had always been mine. It was only a fantasy that someone else was carrying it, ever. I didn't want to think about that.

The scene from the restaurant and the moonlight became more vivid than my new awareness, and I went to sleep thinking about it. I loved the fantasy of romance. Illusion or not, I didn't want it taken from me.

CHAPTER
FIVE

Tuesday, December 14, 1982

My repeated thoughts about romance, moonlight and the restaurant persisted during my walk to Anna's that next morning. I began talking shortly after I walked into the kitchen. She reacted with a consoling hug.

"Every night I look at the Gulf and remember my husband. I know I'm alive when I have feelings. They are my feelings so I can interpret them as any feeling my creative mind can create. Would you like to know what I do with the feeling of loneliness you described? I capture that wonderful feeling. Instead of lonely, I call it *Love.* That's worked for 12 years and it keeps my feelings of love alive. I can share those feelings of love and spread them around in all directions, just like I do the bulbs.

"I've found no market for lonely. It's impossible to sell lonely or give it away. Nobody wants it. I've practiced what I'm preaching for so long that I look forward to that feeling of love in my chest and remember what can't be taken from me. And you can do the same thing. It seems to me that when most of us experience a feeling, the first thing we think about is killing it off or getting rid of it the quickest way we can. I think this is a good time for you to *hold on*. It's certainly not a good time to *let go*.

"Now! Let's talk about the ultimate romantic bond."

Library Habits

She wanted to talk in another room today. We walked through her dining room into a two-story room with a very large skylight. Books on the numerous bookshelves on one wall went all the way to the ceiling.

"Do you have the library habit? If not, get it!" she said.

We sat opposite each other in a well lighted corner of the room near a window. I had a view of a large vacant area with several of the oak trees, yet my eyes returned to an old typewriter on one end of a long table in the center of the room. The typewriter had in it what she'd called her "newest composition." She told me she could still type "crudely" and that her daughter made all the necessary corrections for her.

I asked her why she'd kept all the books since she could no longer read them. Her pithy reply was, "You and I agree that it's good to mingle with living people. Well, it's also good to mingle with the great minds of all ages. I don't have to read them. I just mingle with them.

"I recommend when you read a book that you put yourself in the author's shoes and think another's thoughts. You can come back to your own. Open your mind and entertain all ideas. Keep a dictionary close by and make sure you agree on definitions of words." Anna led into her next question.

A New Look At Synergy

Again she wanted me to define synergy. I knew that she was testing me. After all, I'd read her letter to Rachael. This time, I related it to chemicals or pills and said, "When two chemicals have the desired outcome that neither can have alone, it's synergy. In relationships, it's much the same. We work better together than individually."

I told her I didn't believe a true synergistic relationship happened until later in life because of the personal development that can only come through experience. I was distracted and looked at Anna.

"Anna! Please quit snickering! I'm serious about all this. Most of us didn't luck out. We have to work at it."

"You make it all so impersonal, it's become snicker material!" Anna stated. "I know you can quote experts and talk about internal control. You either speak without experience, or you are incapable of integrating it into what's happening in your life right now. I don't want more theories and neither do you."

"I guess my list of requirements for a synergistic relationship wouldn't impress you?" I tried to be funny.

Anna abruptly said, "No. How is a list of requirements for a synergistic relationship any different from the list you spoke of in other relationships? A shopping list for a special hair color or personality type? No thanks! A shopping list for a person having completed their personal development? I'm 90 years old and I've not completed *my* personal development. That list does not impress me. You do. How does it all relate to you?"

I looked over the list I'd planned to read to her, and silently skimmed through what I'd written. I was almost angry and I felt hurt and scolded. I remembered being a child and holding my breath when I got angry or scolded and going away mentally because I couldn't think. When I got older, I learned to say something, anything, just to keep my mind active until I could regroup my thoughts. Some very irresponsible things came out of my mouth during those years.

I thought about the scrambled egg, and the white of the egg overpowering the yolk and I was pleased with my present reaction. I didn't feel overwhelmed. I'd only been confronted, and I could learn from that.

I remained silent until I could collect my thoughts. "Thanks, Anna, I guess it's time I hear how I'm progressing. I was getting stuck on one word, wasn't I?"

I tore the list of requirements for a synergistic relationship into tiny pieces as I began.

"After the divorce I attended workshops and lectures that related to my work with families of alcoholics — a field in which I'd volunteered and worked for over 20 years. I studied neuro-linguistics and became interested in phobias, especially among alcoholics. I'm still searching and writing about my findings there. I joined an art therapy study group, which included clay sculpting. Most of my social life was spent with friends I'd known for many years who shared many of my interests. Also I helped organize the group of therapists I told you about.

"During that time, I learned a great deal about what I didn't need or want from a romantic partner. I didn't need someone to take care of me financially or physically. I didn't want to cook every day. I didn't want to be in charge of someone's stomach ever again. I'd served my time. I didn't want to work around another person's clock, and I didn't want someone in charge of my time. I didn't want to report in like a school kid. I didn't need his value system or his social life. I learned a great deal about what I didn't need or want but not very much about what I wanted.

"I took a break from romantic relationships altogether and concentrated on my business and my hobbies. I gained a different kind of appreciation for men and for myself. Most of the time now, not always, when another person evaluates me or validates me or mirrors me, I listen. But the ultimate evaluation is my own internal validation system. I'm the only person who knows what I'm attempting to accomplish or how far I've come.

"At some point I began to feel more secure in my lifestyle and confident in my work. I learned that I had something to contribute to others and something to keep for myself, regardless of what happens in any relationship.

My Friend Stan

"During the break from romantic relationships, I met Stan and what friends we have become! We call each other our 'transition' relationship. He and I were getting a divorce about the same time. We decided to be supportive and honest with each other and work at our friendship. We've had our mature and our immature moments together. I've told him how I felt while I was feeling it, and he didn't run away or leave with his feelings hurt. Neither did he leave me when my feelings were hurt. I'm willing to do the same for him. He told me he's been more vulnerable with me than ever, ever." I paused as I felt the same old warm familiar friendship feelings for Stan that had been there since our first meeting.

"I wanted to call him about midnight last night and again this morning, but I decided to talk to you about my feelings instead. I didn't expect from you the same acceptance I would have got from Stan and, you didn't disappoint me!"

Anna said sweetly, "Much better than a list, don't you think? Sorry I have to get so rough, but I get carried away with my theories, too. I need you to stop me also, if you will. We both need a change of pace, and I have a plan. If you're willing to drive us somewhere, we'll have a perfect atmosphere for you to learn what I want you to know about meditation."

We walked to my house, ate a ham and cheese sandwich and then drove a short distance to the tiny Schoenstatt Chapel on a beach. The chapel was small, all alone with a few trees between it and the beach. We were the only people I saw all afternoon. It definitely was a perfect place for meditation. We sat together on a bench that overlooked the Gulf while Anna taught.

Meditation

I listened to her explain how energizing meditating twice a day for about 20 minutes can be. She made me promise not to complicate my meditation the way I had my other training.

"Let your thoughts come and let them go for 20 minutes, preferably the first thing in the morning and immediately after a work day. Make yourself a slave to meditation and

assure yourself of good mental health for life." She giggled,
"Of course, if you are healthy enough to do what is good for
you, you're already pretty healthy mentally. Most people
stop doing it when they find that it's good for them. People
have told me they don't have time to meditate, but I've
observed that they have time for all kinds of stress-related
disorders.

"About noise while you're meditating — just let the noises
relax you more. And your thoughts — if one wants to hang
around a while, let it be. Thoughts that want to go, let them
go. Just let your thoughts come and go. This is one time that
you let Mother Nature do your mind-work. You remember
that fine little discarder, don't you? She'll sort it out for you."

She gave me a mantra which I repeated several times as
she instructed. I was to say the word silently to begin my
meditation and then allow the mantra to come and go as it
pleased while I meditated. But I was never to concentrate on
the mantra or anything else. I was not to say the mantra aloud
again ever. "And don't tell it to a soul," she'd said.

We went into the chapel and meditated. After she opened
her eyes, she sat silently for another ten minutes or so. Later
she told me that she and her husband had come there after
every family crisis or when they wanted to be together in a
different way.

"We found comfort in our silent space together in that little
place," Anna reminisced. "I guess we were lucky in love. We
had all the components of synergism about which you spoke.
I always had my own money, studies, career, friends and
hobbies. Of course, my husband never objected to a thing I
wanted to do. His life was his children and me, and that
made my life just about wonderful. Someone asked me once
if I would ever consider marrying again and I said, 'When my
dog died, I didn't replace him. When my son died, I didn't
replace him. So when my husband died, it never occurred to
me to replace him!' "

End of Fifth Day with Anna

I wanted to hear more about her family, but she wanted to
get home and prepare her lesson plan.

"Tomorrow, you'll become familiar with *agape* and *eros*. I'd like to introduce you to a few new ways to get and give what you will need in all your relationships."

Before she got out of the car, she held both of my hands and said, "Have a better evening. You're going to become such a live wire that nobody will want to step on you."

CHAPTER
SIX

Wednesday, December 15, 1982

Anna said she'd have her lesson planned and be ready for me, and she was.

"So the judge said you were divorced," were her greeting words. "Was your decision to divorce an act of love or the failure of love?" she wanted to know. "Do you know the difference between erotic love and agapic love?"

My head was shaking and turning in all directions, in response to the questions.

"I'm no scholar, but in matters of the heart I refer to eros and agape more often for immediate answers than I refer to any philosophy, religion or psychology," Anna continued. "The Greeks have refined and defined all our loves. They've given names and philosophies to them all, but you and I are going to deal only with eros and agape.

"Let's study in the library today. You'll need some reference books before the day is over." Anna talked and walked quickly into the library. There were several books on the long table in the center of the room. Each of them had book markers and a few yellow highlight marker lines on some of the pages.

She told me, "Those marks, every one of them, were done when I could see. They represent many years of dedicated study. My father said, 'Anna, you won't live long enough to learn it all from experience, so you'd better learn some things from other people.' I hope I've chosen my teachers well.

Eros

"When I hear someone complicate relationships, I make absolutely certain that I hear myself say what I need to hear about eros and agape," Anna said. "It's my way of keeping things simple and down to this earth where I live. Now, listen 'loud.'

"Eros is a desire, an unrelenting desire, to get its needs met. Eros gives of itself willingly, but it always expects something in return.

"Friendship is a good example of eros. We all need a special sharing relationship with another person, but we do expect some return on our investment, don't we?

"All our creativity comes from eros. It's the driving force for personal growth, education and all the arts. It's always striving for its share of truth and beauty, and it's satisfied only for short periods of time. An artist relaxes a short while and then has a creative need to begin something new. Don't you find that true? I believe we're all artists. We're certainly all creative. But when our creativity is squashed, watch out divorce courts and cling clinics!

"Eros is sociable. Aloneness hurts, and eros reaches out. It reaches out because it's lonely, and then it struggles for separation and independence.

"Romantic love is eros. Romantic love must have movement and growth, time together and time apart. What satisfies eros one day doesn't the next. New needs surface and eros once again gets the need met. I love eros. It's what I call earth love.

"Romantic love is fickle and fragile. It can be switched from one person to another. It must have what it needs, and, then, when need is satisfied, need dies. Eros' painful,

frustrating, unending driving force accomplishes its demanding goals and then suffers burn-out.

"Romantic love dies from being left, from neglect, deceit
and abuse. It dies from close examination. It refuses to prove
itself or be detected. If you hire a detective to find it or prove
it, it dies. Romantic love needs stimulation or it dies. And, just
like sexual eros, it's never permanently satisfied.

"Sexual eros is satisfied for a while. But it, too, is soon
revived, just like the artist.

Agape

"We have the capacity for many kinds of love including
agapic love, which is not born of need like eros. Agape gives
of itself and asks nothing in return for its investment. It's self-
generating and never dies. It never gives up, never loses and
never competes. Agape is happy when something or
someone pleases our loved ones. Agape believes that all our
accomplishments add to everyone and everything, and it
knows that sharing a friend is not losing one.

"Agape is unconditional. Try doing a good deed without
getting found out. Find the self-generating power that one
little deed can ignite. If you get found out, the deed doesn't
count. To do a good deed and not get found out is very
difficult. Try not leaving a trace. I'm not talking about not
telling anyone. I'm talking about no one ever knowing who
did the good deed."

"Anna, stop a minute," I pleaded. "Give more examples of
agape. I've always found it a bit too perfect. It's never been
very realistic or earthy enough for me."

Anna said, "Well, some refer to it as God-Love. It's the love
we have for our children. Yes, I know about all the
expectations of parents and that you're ready to argue for
placing parental love into eros. That's not what my example
of agape is all about. You would have to witness a parent who
knows a child has done the gravest of all wrongs, and
observe the parent's never-dying love — painful, yes, but
never-dying love. If you've experienced it, you recognize it.
That's one way I bring agape down to earth.

"Some say it's not of this world. I'm here to tell you it is. It's all around us. It's a free gift." She walked about the room, straightening things, picking up little gift-like items, holding them affectionately.

Combining Eros And Agape

"A blend of agapic and erotic love can mature one faster than anything I know. It takes the edge off emotional greediness. Try it. Try consciously combining eros and agape. Our selfish jealous demands can be blended with an unselfish desire for other people to get what they have coming to them — their share of truth and beauty right along with ours.

"Now you know almost as much as I know about eros and agape. While you read today, you'll find what I'm saying said many different ways by Kierkegaard, Smedes, Durant and others. They've stolen most of my best lines."

Jealousy And Eros

During that day I wanted to know if eros or agape had a solution for jealousy. Therapy brings it out of the shadow, but in most of the male/female relationships I've known, jealousy is rarely absent for very long.

Jealousy is one of the prices we pay for the pleasure of erotic love. She told me that jealousy was the constant companion of romantic love and that the proof was in the knowledge that when love dies, jealousy also dies.

"Lovers are always jealous" she said, "because erotic love, being borne out of need, always fears — and/or feels — the pain of being replaced or losing someone. No one in a romantic relationship is free from jealousy.

"The oneness that we all seek is impossible. There is always the need for separation and independence as well as the need for union with another.

"If you have no interest other than your lover, you can be assured of the worst possible stabbing pains of jealousy."

She emphasized, "Do not narrow your interests until you have only your lover in your life. When you first begin to feel isolation, increase your interests immediately. Take lessons in something; do something. This is a good time to 'triangulize' — get a healthy interest other than your lover. Erotic love refuses to be pushed. To push your lover will kill his romantic love. He is controlled by the same power and has needs other than romantic needs that must be met, just as you have.

"That's how so many people make dreadful mistakes, I believe. When they isolate themselves, they expect the other person to do the same — sure death of erotic love — guaranteed.

"A healthy triangle is a third interest that can absorb the tension and uncertainty of erotic love. There can be no relationship between two people without tension. It's what we do with the tension that makes us different. There are healthy and unhealthy ways to deal with this. Be very, very observant about what you do with tension. First, assume that it exists, then protect yourself.

"One unhealthy way of protecting yourself is to absorb the tension and become responsible for all the unhappiness around you. The tension you absorb will become stored energy that will grow into a physical or mental disability of some kind.

"Another unhealthy way to displace tension is to blame someone other than yourself — your spouse, kids, parents or ancestors. You can also place the blame onto society and justify it with facts — facts that may very well be true. The healthy question is what can we do to correct this nonsense. The cause may be or may not be important. Alcoholics have proven that they don't have to know the cause of their alcoholism to arrest it. They only have to do something about it. That's what I'm saying, we don't have to know the cause of our anxiety to do something about it.

"Some people displace their tension onto the next generation. If you show a child how to deal with tension by taking pills, drinking alcohol, being a tyrant, sulking or being passive, what do you think the child will do when he or she has tension. The same thing you do, of course.

"That's how my ancestors did it. They passed it on to the next generation, and out of that inherited cluster of guilt and responsibility came a lot of physical and mental disorders. Each time they passed it on, the yolk got smaller and the families got more scrambled.

"I lucked out in some ways. I recall in 1906 I was 14 years old and visiting with my cousins in Alabama. One of the boys asked me to beg him not to drink alcohol. Well, you know what I said to him, don't you? 'I don't care what you drink.' He was shocked at my reaction because all the girls begged their boy friends not to do certain things in those days. They called me a rebel from Texas.

"*Your* mother knew she had a rebel on her hands when you wanted to own your own hair, didn't she? Your mother gave you the responsibility for your own hair, and she didn't take it back. She gave you right along with it an opportunity to separate from the scrambled egg. You probably did very well until you got married. If you were like most of us, you didn't know what tension was until you got married. And you and your husband probably dealt with that energy the same way your parents and his parents dealt with theirs.

"I believe that's where some of your fear of an intense relationship is, Miss Zoe. You'll have to decide if I'm correct. It's time to begin learning some healthy ways to displace that lively energy.

Fear And Axiety

"If you don't know the difference between anxiety and fear, it's time. Fear is what you experience when you can see, hear or feel the cause of it, such as a bear lunging toward you. That's fear. Your body reacts to that stimuli immediately and prepares itself for survival. The body doesn't need a lot of intellectual decision-making skills when a bear is coming toward it, so it rushes the chemicals and blood that is normally used for routine functioning into the extremities for action.

"Anxiety is not so easy to detect. We can't see it or hear it or touch it and it can have an unknown cause. However, the body doesn't know the difference from anxiety or fear, and it prepares itself in the same way. When we are anxious, we are in a state of readiness much like we are when a bear is lunging toward us. That's why we can't think when we are anxious — the body is prepared to flee or fight.

"Learning to deal with our anxiety and reduce that tension in some healthy ways can have some far reaching benefits — into all the generations to come. The roots of our family tension tree grow very deep.

"Think of what we can do with all our phobias if we understood our bodies well enough to learn some healthy ways to reduce our anxiety. Meditation, talking about our anxiety and feelings and taking responsibility for our minds and bodies is a start.

"Additionally, to triangle into a healthy outside interest is very important. Healthy couples find relief in any number of common interests. Some have found it in a church or a 12-step program. Find a power greater than your lover. That's what I suggest — and I don't believe I'm the first one to think of that suggestion.

"I've wandered off my track a little, so let's get back to eros and agape and when they change from one to the other.

When Eros Becomes Agape

"What may begin as romantic love can become agapic, I believe. How else can you explain the love a woman has for an alcoholic husband? It's obvious her erotic love for him is dead. Yet she has no desire to hurt him. What kind of love is that? I think it's agapic love, God-like love. Sometimes she chooses to divorce him. Sometimes she chooses not to divorce him. Couldn't either decision be an act of love?

"It takes courage, love and lots of faith to divorce or stay with a chemical. It's not the person about which she has trouble making a decision. She did that a long time ago. It's the chemical — the appendage to him that she detests. Losing a lover to another person or to death is painful, but losing a loved one to a chemical, such as alcohol or cocaine, can be equally devastating.

"We are now back to my first question this morning about your decision to divorce. Was your decision to divorce an act of love or the failure of love?

"Don't answer, just listen," Anna requested.

Decisions

Anna continued enthusiastically. "Decision-making needs eros, agape and flexibility. To make any decision about anything, you must take it one day at a time and go as far as you can see. From there, you can see all you need to see.

"When I first heard that, I thought of going on a trip. If I try to think of every possible thing that may happen, I'd never leave home. When I begin a trip and go only as far as I can see — to the first intersection, stop and look both ways — from there I can see farther. If there's an accident on the street I'd planned to turn onto, the decision is easy. I can take another street.

"All decisions are about that simple if we chunk them down into manageable sizes. We don't have to make all our decisions about the trip before we leave home. Don't expect to work out all the details of any one decision, ever! Do you understand? In fact, a good life has to have flexibility planned into it, I believe." She was silent for a long time which allowed me time to think about what she had just said.

Anna wanted me to study alone for the remainder of the day. "You just might find some missing link between your Love, Santa and God. Keep bringing samples of your writing. See you tomorrow, same time," she said and closed the library door.

I was to take notes from all her books on eros and agape.

End of Sixth Day with Anna

Reverberating across the chasms of theories on relationships, Anna's lessons began to connect them all.

The days were speeding by much too fast. I'd have only five more days with Anna. Her knowledge and 90 years of experience were freely given. When I asked whether she was as tired as I, she said, "When you learn what you came here to learn, you will no longer be tired. You know I have to give it away to keep it. Everybody knows that!"

Before going to bed that night I wrote about how much lighter my bundle felt after reviewing eros and agape through Anna. I knew that jealousy would never feel the same again.

Several times during that day I remembered a letter I'd written to a man I'd been obsessed with once upon a time. I searched through several stacks of letters before I found it. In it I had allowed the child within me to do the talking. I didn't want to discount that letter or its importance another minute.

Love From Me To You

I want to tell you about what happened Saturday night. We were trying to go to sleep, and I was crying softly, trying to be quiet, but the tears came out anyway. Instead of discounting me as she does sometimes, she wiped the tears gently and acknowledged me and my love for you. She had told me many times why you can't be with us. She said we mustn't be envious of those other than us who make you happy. We should be happy that they can share a part of you that we can't. She told me that you love us even though you can't be with us. She had said all this so often in the past I expected to hear it again.

Before she had a chance to talk, I told her that I was trying to remember what she had taught me; and I wanted to believe her. I would like to be mature and forgiving and happy for someone other than me, but I'm not always. There are times when I forget and cry for no reason that I know.

I told her I wanted to be with you and hold you and feel your presence and hear your voice and be certain that you really are okay and that you really are happy being away. Saturday night she surprised me. She said, "I understand." She didn't try to reason with me. She let the tears fall, and she hugged me affectionately. She said she wanted the same thing that I wanted. We went to sleep hugging each other because neither of us knew what to do. It hurt me to see her cry so hard. I never knew that we both loved you.

That's the reason I want to write to you. She will never tell you about Saturday night. When you call or come to see us, we both get excited and enjoy your time with us so much that we don't want to spoil it by making you sad. She'd scold me for sneaking this note to you. We're supposed to find a way to handle it ourselves, she'd say. Maybe you'd best not tell her about it. But if I didn't know that she loves you — maybe you don't either.

Love to You from ME.

After reading that letter a few times, I reviewed Anna's egg yolk and egg white theory and all my family systems training. That letter contained the adult reasoning of the egg yolk and the child's raw emotions of the egg white trying to communicate with each other. It also helped me to separate God-love from romantic love and the importance of what we teach and have been taught.

My bundle was different after that day.

CHAPTER
SEVEN

Thursday, December 16, 1982

During breakfast Anna decided that my voice was sad and she wanted to know if I knew why. She didn't miss the opportunity to tell me that discussing feelings doesn't change them, but talking about feelings will reduce the anxiety. Within that tension-free time we then have access to our own reasoning ability as well as feedback from the person we are trusting with our feelings.

I said, "Anna, it's the 16th of December. Our time is going much too fast for me. You give and give and I still want more. I want to hold tight to the feeling I have in your presence, and I don't want it to end. I'm spoiling my present time by thinking ahead. Perhaps I need advanced classes in letting go of my letting-go lessons!"

"Are you talking about that deep emotional breath-holding feeling?" Anna asked. "The one that feels good and warm and wants to cuddle and wallow inside yourself? The feeling of being fed everything it needs?"

I admitted she was right on target.

"I'd love to keep you in my womb of wisdom," she laughed. "We'll practice all our letting-go lessons soon enough. For now let's enjoy being aware of the death of the minutes."

We talked about yesterday's lesson, worked in her yard until mid-morning then Anna said, "Let's go in now. I have some things for us to do today. Look in my notebook, and you'll find a section on Changes. But I won't listen to another word without a walloping big bowl of Blue Bell ice cream. Let's walk out to the end of the pier and eat it. You also brought your homework, I'm assuming. I can't wait! More about you!"

She began singing, "Getting to Know you. Getting to Know All About You," then said to me, "Be sure to protect your papers from the wind. It can get pretty breezy, where we're off to."

Crab Pier

Tiny and fast — everything she did she hurried to and through.

Anna asked me to carry the ice cream she had put into the large bowls.

We were out the door, across the street and on the pier within minutes. Anna was raising crab lines as we went along. I juggled the ice cream and file folder while I listened to her.

"I never have to do anything but raise these lines and put the crabs in a live box. Someone other than me baits them. On weekends we have a crab boil and tell crab stories. See what happens when you hold on too long!" she said and pulled a line with two crabs on one bait. She dipped into the water with a long-handled net and in a flash put them into a crab trap.

The end of the pier had a protected, cozy area with two cushioned chairs, a large light and a fan in the ceiling. I placed the ice cream and folder on a table and joined Anna.

She said, "My kids won't hear of me coming out here alone. I could do it, you know. I just don't want to disobey anyone. Guess they may be right — sometimes the wind wants to blow me away. Now just what could you do if I fell in the water right here?"

"I'd stand on my tiptoes and talk you back to safety just like you did for your friend, Mava. Or maybe I would throw you a crab line and pull you in if you could hold on tight enough!"

Anna smiled, "You may be learning too much. An analogy proceeds on the unsound assumption that if two or more things agree with one another in some respect, they will agree in other respects. When it comes to me, I hope you'll have the wisdom to know the difference!"

We were having so much fun we were both slightly out of breath. Inside the shed we looked at the melted ice cream and started giggling again. Anna said, "Now we are the blue belles! Oh well, it isn't so much what's on the table that matters, as what's on the minds of what's in the chairs. This ice cream would be good boiled." She drank the bowl of cream without taking it from her mouth.

Anna said, "I've been wanting to say that I'm happy you are a sculptress. That impresses me. I guess George Bernard Shaw said it best. He thought the sculptor must have something of the god in him. According to GBS, from the sculptor's hand comes a form which reflects a spirit. He said the sculptor does not sculpt to please us or to please himself but because he must. Do you believe that?" she asked.

"I call it clay play. Sculptress sounds a little sophisticated for what I do," I responded.

"Start by giving yourself a title. Do you believe what GBS said?" Anna insisted, "Don't prevaricate and don't procrastinate. Don't prevaricate about something you do well by belittling it. If you do something well, say so. And don't procrastinate about doing it."

Art Therapy

I said, "I've never known where some of my art pieces come from. Pleasing anyone, including myself, never occurs to me. An example of what you're saying is in a series that I

call 'The Freeing of a Woman.' I worked until I was
exhausted without a goal in mind. At the time I had no idea
it had a thing to do with freedom.

"Irene, an art therapist, wouldn't allow us to project on
another's art work. She said anything we said about another
person's art was a projection of ourselves and that we were
telling about ourselves when we critiqued.

"Irene freed me to work without worrying about what
someone else thought. I no longer concerned myself about
art rules or anatomical exactness. I can't reproduce the
pieces and every one is one of a kind."

I continued. "There's a lot of talk today about finding
answers from within ourselves about our past, present and
future.

"One of the keys to that information is in the therapy of
art, I believe. I start squeezing clay with no art object in
mind. I just go with it. I enjoy using two colors when I'm in
conflict about something and I allow each color to be one
side of an issue. When I get my problem outside myself, I
see more than my solution to my dilemma. There's always
the unknown. It's also a fascinating way to communicate
with friends and especially with children. I like the part
about projections best of all. Anything any one has to say
about my clay or art work is telling me about them, not
about me."

Writing Art

Anna said, "If you will remember that about your writing,
too, you can be just as free to say what you want said. When
we get our thoughts outside ourselves, we can begin to
make some order of them. The power of our thoughts has
little to do with the number of our thoughts, but in the order
of them. Thoughts are not limited to the educated people.
Everyone thinks, so it's not the number of the thoughts you
want to concern yourself with but the order you make of
them.

"I can't think of a better way to begin to organize your
thoughts than to see them on paper. Your Irene was right.

When we read what another person has written, we are limited to our own experiences, and we project only that much. I want to hear some of your writing. I can't see your sculptures, but I can hear your writing art.

"We came out here to talk about changes, didn't we?" Anna began her questions. "Letting go of time, isn't that what you asked? What about the changes you experience when you read some of your private life to me? When you share your life with me, I know it's a gift. And what's my gift today?" She squeezed my hand as she asked.

I held my letters close to my body. I said, "Anna, the following two letters were written at a time that you will understand as I read to you. When I wrote the letter to Linda, I had no idea what would follow."

Letter To Linda

Dearest Linda, my friend and my confidant, good morning,

I want to attempt to tell you how I feel about our years together and my investment in your family. You and I agree that when we get involved with a person we begin to call a friend, it's like going to a movie. We begin to see the surroundings, hear the sounds and we get emotionally involved with the characters. We want to know the outcome and we usually hang around until the end. My investment and involvement in your family movie has happened over a 20-year period of time.

Linda, I know that your husband and my dear friend, Mark, will soon become a memory. A heart attack, a blood clot and he was brain dead two years ago at the age of 48. Life is so fleeting, and people touch us for such a second in time, it's difficult to know we've been touched until it's too late. I'd like to tell Mark, but it's too late for that.

I'm also thinking of his sister. I want to call her and acknowledge her loss but the stabbing pain from my two sisters' deaths keeps me away from her. Each time I want to acknowledge her pain, I feel my own pain. It hurts so much that I do nothing. I have other sisters and other loved ones who are not dead. I need to tell them all how I feel; and so, I'm starting with you and your sons, Marcus and Erick.

Do you remember the stick story that you and I liked so much? The author is unknown but here it is again:

The Cold Within

Six humans trapped by happenstance
in black and bitter cold
Each one possessed a stick of wood,
Or so the story's told.

Their dying fire in need of logs,
The first man held his back,
For on the faces around the fire
He noticed one was black.

The next man, looking across the way,
Saw one not of his church,
And couldn't bring himself to give
The fire his stick of birch.

The third man sat in tattered clothes
He gave his coat a hitch.
Why should he put his log to use
To warm the idle rich.

The rich man just sat back
And thought
Of the wealth he had in store,
And how to keep what he had earned
From the lazy, shiftless poor.

The black man's face
Bespoke revenge,
As the fire passed from sight;
For all he saw in his stick of wood
Was a chance to spite the white.

The last man of this forlorn group
Did naught except for gain,
Giving only to those who gave
Was how he played the game.

Their logs held tight
In death's still hands
Was proof of human sin.
They didn't die from the cold without;
They died from the cold within.

And here we are, Linda, caught by happenstance in the black
and bitter cold of the reality of Mark's death — the cold and bitter

reality of having to swallow life's painful experiences. How do we keep the fire burning? How do we put our stick of wood on the fire to keep it alive?

I no longer want to be trapped by happenstance, prejudice, religion, worn out beliefs, money and clothes: mine or yours or theirs. I no longer want to be trapped by judgments, spitefulness or fear of future insecurity. Neither do I want to wait for others to give first, holding tight to my love.

Each time you and I talk about the ending of your time with Mark, I'm reminded of the ending of my marriage to Madison and what great friends the four of us were.

When I hear you talk about what you could have done differently with Mark, I'm reminded of the following story that Madison gave me in 1963.

On Being Sad And Glad

'Several horsemen were crossing a stream at night when a voice instructed them to dismount and fill their pockets with the pebbles in the water. In haste, they only took a few, whereupon came the dawn and behold, they realized the rocks were diamonds. They were glad they had got as many as they had, but sad they had not taken more when they had the opportunity.'

Linda, I'm feeling awfully sad and I want to remember the glad as well. I want you to know how much I love you and how many diamonds I carry with me. Our experiences when we were so young seemed to have been pebbles at the time. But now that Mark and Madison are in a different place, each of the memories have turned into magnificent diamonds for me. I, too, would have done many things differently with Madison as well as with all my other loved ones. But it's too late to go back now. All I can do is treasure my diamonds and put another stick on the fire, I guess.

Thanks for being one of the main characters in the movie of my life. It hurts to hurt with you, but it hurts more to hurt without you. Let's stay close.

Love,
Zoe

Letter To Patsy

To my dear Sister Patsy,
Too late to write, but can't not write. I was reading over my letter to Linda at the time you died. When I got to the place about

my deceased sisters, I couldn't continue reading. I thought about
you so intensely and what I needed to say to you.

The rain last night made me very, very sad. I couldn't not think
about you and me in the rain at the gentle ages of five and seven.
You, with your infinite wisdom, saving me from the elements. I
felt safe with you.

I remembered a time when you and Daddy were fishing several
miles away, and a storm came. The current, the enormous rain, the
waves, the fear I saw in Mama's eyes have remained implanted.
When you and Daddy finally came in, we had already had to leave
our flooded home. What a relief when we saw the two of you so
rain-drenched. I couldn't love you enough. I recall promising
myself that I would never again be angry with you. I would let you
play with my dolls, even the one with the eyes that opened when
I laid her down. Then within 15 minutes, you had done something
that made me take back all my promises.

Last evening, these were some of my thoughts. They were bits
and pieces of scenes with you and me. You became a registered
nurse, married a physician and had four children. Then your
alcoholism and the pain you couldn't handle. You were too
sensitive a soul for this old world, weren't you?

I'll think about you an awful lot today. I just hope that I can
remember to be both sad and glad. I'll give you a special send
off . . . I loved you . . . I admired you . . . I thought you were the
most beautiful sister, and I was so proud of you.

Love,

Zoe

P.S. I still am!

Apology To Linda

Dear, dear Linda,

As I dragged my heavy bones in the door, the phone was
ringing. Erick, your now-grown up son, gave me the message.
Mark had died last night. I couldn't handle any more. I began to
feel spacey . . . I couldn't hold on to anything, or be with you as
I wanted to . . . I was tired from Patsy's funeral and the six hours
of driving. That was a stressful time for me, and yet I've never
forgiven myself for not giving more to you when you needed me.

Love,

Zoe

Anna reached for both my hands, squeezed them gently and said, "I love you. Can you feel it?"

Anna could sum it all up with a touch. I'd been writing and throwing away my writings since childhood, but I was still uncomfortable reading them to anyone.

Anna said, "I believe writing is the most therapeutic thing we can do during or after a crisis. The very effort to state your ideas and feelings on paper helps to clear them up, as you already know.

"Keep writing. If a musician or composer must practice, why shouldn't a writer. Write in the style you prefer, and soon your thoughts will begin to think in that style on paper. Practice writing what you think, and particularly do so in the matters about which you're confused. Once, my husband asked me how I knew when to write. I said, 'You know when to go to the bathroom, don't you?' It was just about that urgent and demanding. I had to write!"

Anna continued. "When you begin to write whatever you are writing — a letter, a speech, poetry or a book — it's all the same question. What is your intent? And, what is the intent of your next writing? I'm ready."

"Anna, the next letter is about changes and adapting to change. Maybe it was meant to inform myself. Now don't you laugh! It was a giant step for me."

I began reading something I had written to all my friends *the day I got old.*

Changes

I'm experiencing a change within myself today. I've not yet accepted what I need to accept but I feel "it" pushing me.

What I speak of is my age. I want to hold on, but I know I must give up my youth — accept that I am now leaving my youth behind. I must live out my life remembering what I didn't know to treasure.

I know that I must move on. I need to accept the changing season, the changing me — go on to another level of life and read my AARP magazine. There has to be life after AARP — or is there? How will I ever know if I don't experience the loss?

I just cried a bucket of tears as I looked in the mirror and saw myself for the first time in years. The hands are wrinkled like the face. I know there are face lifts and hand lifts and tummy tucks and spot removers, but who would I be fooling?

I've heard that we have two lives — one we learn with and one we learn to live with what we learned with.

I won't know what I have learned until I accept where I am today, who is in my life and what and who is important to me.

To be thankful for what I had, what I had taken from me and what I have left will take quite an inventory. With a bit of searching, I came across you. What do I have left? You were in that file. For you I am grateful and just wanted to say so.

I need you and time is running on. I want to say "I love you" to people I love more often than I've said it in the past. I may not always have the time. Thanks for being in my life. You are, you know. Thanks for letting me share what's left of me as I begin the boiling-down process.

Please stay in touch. I need reassuring more. I get busy, too, and forget. But never a day goes by that I don't remember a special moment with you, and I want there to be more. What will we have as we get older still — if we don't get them now.

Put me in your "moments to remember" file. You're being held with deep affection in mine.

Love,
Zoe

Anna didn't laugh. I looked closely for her response. Her brows wrinkled but her face smiled. Og Mandino tells a great story about our body being the greatest miracle on earth. Looking at Anna, I saw that miracle. Her skin had repaired itself, and it had held her together for 90 years. For me to have worried about something so mundane as wrinkles instead of what was inside the wrinkles was the kind of youth I no longer needed.

I was feeling my immaturity when Anna said, "That makes me want to laugh and cry. I laugh because of our age difference. I'm twice as old as you, yet you sound so much older than I feel. I want to cry because I couldn't hold on to time whether I was aware of its importance or not. I feel more helpless because I can't teach you how to hold on to time. It seems to go faster as you learn to value it more . . .

End of Seventh Day with Anna

"Let's go in now. My family is asking for my time this afternoon. We'll come back out here tomorrow if the weather permits. And don't forget to bring more of your writing."

CHAPTER

EIGHT

Friday, December 17, 1982

We were on the pier immediately after breakfast. Anna wanted me to read a letter that Laura had written after a two-year relationship with a man. Anna explained, "Laura didn't tell me all the details, just that she and her lover had planned to have a thing together for a summer, then end it. Laura writes about her feelings every day."

Anna whispered the first gossip I'd heard from her. "Between you and me, it's still going on. I don't know what she'd tell you. When she lets me read part of her book, I think I'm peeking because I know it's true."

Dying Love From OUR SUMMER THING

As I experience the ending of our summer together, I'm sad. I know a big something is dying as surely as the trees are losing their leaves. I can see the leaves. I don't have to guess. There is change and another season approaching. There's the known and the unknown.

I don't know what plants and trees will make it through the winter. I don't know what new growth will be taking place or what has already been planted for the new season.

I'm feeling a difference. My own feelings. I don't have to guess about them. Sad, hurt, painful, yes, but different somehow from all the other hurts. This one has been so very special.

To survive the winter of our relationship, I must move on so there will be something alive of me to bloom after all my leaves have shed, after all my pretenses and hopes have dropped.

What will grow from our summer? What will I have learned? What will I do with the tears? How will I prune myself?

Can I continue to want to grow and to have faith that I will withstand the painful nakedness of the cold? The stripping of my pride? Down to the unmasked unknowns? See myself without blooms? Without color and let others see me?

What will be left? Have I fertilized? Have I been willing to prune both the dead and the living enough to assure myself that life has to be lost in order for new life to be born again? Will I be willing to cut this relationship off while there is still life in the relationship? Or will I hold tight to the little life that is left and kill the whole thing?

Will I be honest with you? Will I have the courage to risk moving on to another kind of relationship with you? Will I risk an ending, risk you and me without illusion, without hope for us together?

I have just experienced my last full moon without you. I finally got the message. You won't be experiencing them with me. You haven't been, but I always thought that you would share the next one with me. Another lonely Sunday. Another lonely weekend. Another free weekend. Hurt, sad, no telephone call. No, nothing, not a crumb.

It's dying, my special one. Can you see the changing of the season?

Love,
Laura

During the reading of that letter, Anna looked at the water without expression. When I completed the reading, I walked out of the shed to leave her with her silence. I pulled in the crab lines, put my catch into the large live well, and returned to the shed. Anna was still in deep thought so I sat quietly and meditated.

The next thing I heard was Anna's unusually soft voice saying, "I'm back now. Read what you want me to hear."

I said, "I've been carrying the next writing around with me for several days. I wrote it at a time when I didn't know what to do with my feelings. I don't know what to do with the feelings I have for Laura's writing. I'm feeling her message here and here and here," I said as I put my hand on my throat and chest and abdomen.

Feeling Worshippers

Good Morning, Feeling Worshippers:

I've been worshipping a feeling.

One more important than my home, my physical or my mental health.

It has to be valuable. This feeling is in the bottom of the lung area, extending into the rib cage.

I worship this feeling so much that when it's present, I can't function.

This feeling stops me from talking, it stops me from paying my bills and making money to pay my bills.

It stops me from telling you not to do something to me that is harmful.

This feeling stops me from asking someone for something I need or want.

This feeling is precious, very dear to me. It has to be. It costs so much. That is why I treasure it so. I actually worship it.

I have another feeling, not quite so valuable, but possibly related. It's in the center of my throat. When it's present, I talk and talk and talk myself out of whatever I want.

This feeling is precious, very dear to me. It has to be. It costs so much. That's why I treasure it so. I actually worship it.

Another one is in my head. Now this one is truly a treasure. When it's there, I scream, I panic, I allow it to rule my entire body. It is boss. It's overwhelming.

This feeling is precious, very dear to me. It has to be. It costs so much. That's why I treasure it so. I actually worship it.

And, jealousy, I've worshipped it all my life. It keeps me from competing. It keeps me in relationships with inferiors. If you are less than me, how can you hurt me?

*This feeling is precious, very dear to me. When it's present, I have
to ignore it. You would think me inferior to have such a feeling.*

When I ignore it, it gets bigger. This feeling is now larger than
me.

I have no choice but to treasure it. It owns me. I actually
worship it.

I don't have a thing more valuable than my feelings. They're
protecting me. They want something for me.

I can't talk with you today. I'm worshipping my feelings.

Good Morning, Feeling Worshippers!

Be careful where you go for help. There are lots of feeling
worshippers' helpers out there who want you to feel your feelings.

They don't know what to do about them, so they put you in a
larger feeling cage.

Look for one who knows there is vision, taste, smell and
hearing, as well as feelings.

Move out of that small circle.

The world is a beautiful picture. Can you see it?

Love,
Zoe

"You're saying there's a way out of our feelings when
we're a prisoner to them? Hurray! I've always said the same
thing."

"Sure," I said, with a new confident voice, "There's a way.
I have a friend named Marvin. He recently asked me a
question about depression. This is what I gave him."

Whales Of Depression

Dear Marvin:

AND what do I do when I'm depressed? What do I do when I
feel lower than whale manure? What I've done for many years is to
inventory my life when I am up, not when I'm down. I have
definite needs, and when one of them is suppressed, I get down.
I do a quick inventory and learn what's missing. Then all I have to
do is add that ingredient and 'Voila!' That's what works when I
realize I'm headed down. Sometimes it may only be that I'm
expending too much energy in one direction. If that is true, I do
the opposite for a while.

However, there are those times when I'm there before I know it. It takes a lot more doing at those times to dust myself off. I have tremendous respect for my depressions. They always force me beyond where I am. Painful, frustrating — all and more of the words you already know. But, respect also I have for them.

Depression takes more energy than moving the muscles, and moving the muscles is a must when I'm depressed. The sooner I move the muscles, the sooner I get some of the edges in perspective. Diet is important, hormones another, weather, people, all things play a part maybe — who knows? The question is the same. What does one do? I choose to go through mine drug-free and zap them for all they are worth. My depressions almost always are trying to do something for me.

It's like going through a tunnel with no light at the end. If I give myself time and have a little faith, the other side is always different and much brighter once I get through the struggle. Or I can blame myself and others, and the fight might push me through. But most of the time, a little introspection and a good friend is the best and fastest way.

I continue to ask myself, "What is this feeling trying to do for me?" When I don't try to get rid of it, when I recognize it and accept it as useful, I'm amazed at the information I get from myself. From the answer to the question will come other questions and other answers. There's always a part that doesn't want to turn loose of the "old" depressed feeling. That part, too, is trying to do something for me.

I try to think of depressions being full of information saying something is wrong. Most of all they refuse to take any more abuse. They sit down and demand to be heard, felt and seen. Would we ever acknowledge them if they weren't so demanding?

Depressions are like children in need of recognition. If we don't recognize them, they continue to rear their little — not so pretty — parts and will do so at some importunate moments. Without recognition — or worse still — drinking or drugging them away, they get larger and larger and rule us. Depression, once recognized and properly attended to, will give us unbelievable rewards as does the child. We can gain from the experience of depression. We can have a marvelous companion, one we can have faith in, one who will not allow us to get off course for too long because it will again rear its parts for recognition.

That's what I do, dear Marvin.

Love,
Zoe

Resentments

I heard myself beginning to speak like Anna, "Do you know where the word resentment comes from? It comes from the French word 'sentir' meaning 'to feel.' When you add 're,' which means 'again,' you get 'resentir.' From that, we got the word resentment. When you re-feel, you resent.

"Choose a resentment, a feeling that you experience again and again. Deal with the negative feelings or those no longer accomplishing their original purpose. All our feelings at one time had a positive function, and we anchored them in at that time. They've been dutifully performing their original purpose since the time they were anchored.

"Learn some new ways to communicate with your feelings. Make friends of them, ask them questions. They'll no longer be strangers. You can ask them any number of creative questions. You can gain a massive amount of confidence being in control of what has been controlling you all your life. You can get the original anchor to accomplish its pur-pose by giving you an updated solution."

"Are you saying that you have the answers in that little computer between your ears?" she asked and pulled both my ears.

I smiled and continued to teach. "Are you aware that you anchored in your message when you pulled my ears? When you want me to get a message, you anchor the message with a special touch. I thought you'd like to know what you're doing if you don't know how brilliant you are!"

"How brilliant I am," Anna laughed. "I've always told my students to develop confidence in their own brain, not another's brain. I don't always know why something works, but when it does work, I do it again. When it doesn't work after a few times, I stop. Now is that brilliant?"

"If wisdom is brilliance," I answered.

"Lady Zoe, it's time to go in now for a long nap. I've had my fun in the sun and wind. You're becoming a special friend to me, you know. Some people have 'snap;' you have 'snap back.' Take Laura's name and telephone number. Send your writing to her on 'Feeling Worshippers.' She can use it in her work. Take the notebook with you tonight and read the section on 'Friendships.' Read it over the weekend. Take your time and give me a summation of the entire chapter on Monday. I look forward to our time together each day. Would you like to be my new best friend?" she asked with a little girl grin.

We walked back to the house in silence holding hands. Anna went directly to her answering machine. I straightened the kitchen, washed dishes, filed Laura's writings, and got my assignment for Monday ready. I could hear Anna's answering machine all over the house. Students, friends, family, maintenance people, male and female — all had love and excitement in their voices when they talked to Anna.

End of Eighth Day with Anna

I waved and left. I had a Friday afternoon and weekend free and all I could think of was reading Anna's notebook.

CHAPTER

**Saturday and Sunday,
December 18 and 19, 1982**

Saturday's weather was a light-sweater day, a perfect temperature to sit in a swing tied to one of the trees behind my December home. There had been very little pruning or care of these fine old oaks. I easily related Laura's "Dying Summer" letter to the trees and to myself as I held a little tighter to the folder from Anna's notebook of lives.

She'd regretted not keeping more letters from her friends.

"Letters can be a comfort when the person is no longer available, and that day will come if you live long enough. If you're not keeping them, start!" she'd instructed me. The "Friendship" folder was organized like all the other sections and contained the following:

Faultfinding Reflects Self
Thomas a Kempis, 1380-1471

A vulture will fly over a sweet-scented flower garden to seize a stinking carion.

In like manner, the critic passes over many beautiful qualities in search of a fault. He has developed the habit. His captious eyes have warped his view. His satisfaction comes from assailment.

The faultfinder is never a favorite. He is not appreciated. No statue is ever erected to him. The world knows his judgment of others is only a reflection of his own state.

That he has a knocking fist instead of a helping hand, and that he would serve a better cause if he would change his ways and be a model. Such as everyone is inwardly, so he judgeth outwardly.

Woman-To-Woman Abuse

(Anna, 1927) "We women, how we abuse each other, and so covertly. Viciously ignoring and criticizing each other; rarely acknowledging that she is only you or me in another skin with another face and body. Rarely dealing with our jealousy, we just find someone to comfort and agree with us. Will we ever deal with woman-to-woman abuse?"

Letter To Helen

Dear Helen:

Sweetheart, the feelings you have today will not be the same feelings you will have tomorrow. You said your heart is breaking because of Jim's treatment of you and that you've been through this before, which makes this pain tougher to take.

You said you had been repeating over and over to yourself to distrust every thought that you have formed in heat of any kind, and you are reminding yourself that thoughts made under the influence of anger or strong affection need to be set aside to cool. You told me you were afraid these wouldn't cool.

There's such a desperateness to everyone now. Everyone seems to be saying, "This one has to be it." There's no time to allow the relationship to ripen. Everyone just keeps switching partners.

Helen, I believe that therapy is too cheap. We think we can buy it. It's available everywhere. You can have it in private, group or family and for various periods of time. There is every possible language being used including the conscious, unconscious and layers beyond that, according to some, including the collective and psychoid unconscious.

I believe we should get all the therapy we need. I'm in no way discounting what any of us do in the name of friendship, love or therapy. Mother Nature is so simple. Why are we so complicated?

I know you need me and I feel helpless. I'm searching for words that will comfort you. You said, "Nothing works." Helen, dear, do you have faith in your most recent search for therapy, your new church? To sit back and feel the feelings and have faith is a bit much to ask of one's self, but for me, there is comfort when I do it.

You have given me worlds of comfort, help, love, kindness and friendship when I've needed it through many crises for many years, and I love you for being with me every time.

I want to be here for you. But, most of all, I want you, Helen, my old friend, to know that you already have everything you need. You've forgotten, that's all.

Love,
Anna

On a page by itself: "Believe the best, rather than the worst. You will always be right, either way. People have a way of living up — or down — to your opinion of them."

Letter To Dolores

Dear Dolores,

Let those tears wash away your fears, my treasured friend, Dolores. Let them clean the smudges and grit from your perspective and free you to live and love. Let those tears mend and bind and open your vision to unknown insights.

My friend, you just learned that your ex-husband, a man to whom you were married 23 years until six months ago, is to be married soon to a woman he has known less than a year.

You said you haven't quit loving him, you never had the love you wanted from him, your dream of forever just died, you feel raw and that she has won what you never had.

You asked me how long is forever — until the death of the person? Until the death of Love?

Your questions remind me of a song. Some of the words are, "Where does love go when it leaves us, and we won't know the answer, 'til we find it again."

I'd like to fix your hurt. I know you're crying this minute, and I want for you what you want. I hurt when you hurt. I get angry with your enemies. Crushed is crushed and I know you are crushed. My little sister said, "The soft velvet beauty of the butterfly wing can be crushed by the careless touch of sincere love as easily as it can be crushed by a bold fist."

You need for me to be gentle with you, so all I can think to do is to take your hand and look around the scary corners with you.

You asked me about letting go. I believe that letting go too soon is just as harmful as holding on too long. I want to encourage you to hold on and feel what you need to feel and treasure your ability to feel what you are feeling at the time you are feeling what you are feeling. You can't marry away your feelings; neither can he.

Like you told me once, tie a knot and hang on. I'd like to add to that. Untie the knot and drift in space for a while. I'm here to catch you. You can't go too far because I'm with you, and I won't let you do anything too, too foolish. I'll bring this letter with me and have you read it to me. We'll get through this together. I'll be with you while you're alone with your pain.

I love you, Dolores,

Anna

ABOUT TODAY

To my husband and best friend:
Hold my heart a little tighter,
It's older now and can't stand alone.
Let me hold my arms
Around you more,
They need to be fuller now.
Tell me more often you love me,
'Cause time is running away,
And, we may not be able to say —
How happy we've been — or —
About Today.

Love,
Anna

Letter To Jeanne

Dear Jeanne,

While reading some of Helen Keller's words recently, I was reminded of you when she said, "To have known you I count it one of the sweetest privileges of my life. Beautiful flower, you have taught me to see a little way into the hidden heart of things."

My precious next door neighbor friend died of leukemia recently. I want to share a letter I wrote to her the morning following her death. I know you'll understand it.

Dear Rubye:

They tell me you died last night. My silence, grief and anger come together when I look out of my front door and see . . .

The trail between our homes that got larger and larger through the years,

Expanded and shortened by your four-year-old grand-daughter, Stephanie.

Her little toes, barefoot, afraid of Jack Frost.

You would call and tell me she was on her way, 'cause you had made her mad.

She would be so proud, "I traveled by myself," she would say.

Yes, the trail between our homes did get bigger, didn't it.

With Larry and Charlie, your sons,

Your loved ones becoming mine for a moment, and mine — yours.

Once when you were so very sad, we sat in your living room looking at the trail between our homes,

You said how comforting it had become when you couldn't sleep,

You could sit in your living room and be reminded of our friendship and our trail built by you, me and our loved ones.

Rubye, what will happen to our trail, our path? What will happen to our friendship?

I'm hurting this morning.

I have a special sadness and loneliness as I look out my front door and know that you won't be using it any more.

I feel so helpless when I tell your kids and family and friends:

The trail that we all made between our homes is open to you. It's a path made with lots of love, hurt and sharing. It, too, will die, if you don't use it.

Love,
Anna

Jeanne, the bridge or trail that we are building is important to me. I'm just as involved with your kids and love them in special ways, just as I do Larry and Charlie.

Write me one of your long, long letters, Miss Jeanne.

I almost said "call me," and then I remembered you don't have one of those things. As my Dad said, "That land in West Texas is so dry, you'd probably have to fertilize a telephone pole to make a phone call." Is that true? If not, prove it!

Love,
Anna

Letter To Leona

Dear Leona,

Gentle sweetness. I think that's what you represent to me: gentle sweetness. Do you think we choose our friends because of the qualities we possess or those qualities we don't possess? Wouldn't it be nice if gentle sweetness was something I had not acknowledged about myself? I feel gentle and kind, but often come across a bit crusty, I fear.

You and I are to be working on a project soon. I look forward to seeing you more than completing the project, and the project is an endeavor of my life's love work.

In one of Helen Keller's narratives she said, "My friends have made the story of my life. In a thousand ways they have turned my limitations into beautiful privileges, and enabled me to walk serene and happy in the shadow cast by my deprivation."

Before I leave you, I want to ask you to dig out what you have on Mortimer J. Adler. I like to call him a re-educator, leading the research on The Great Books concept of learning through group discussion. His goal was to re-direct the thinking of educators back to previous centuries — those writings that have survived the times.

I love it when Adler takes on Socrates. He said, "Socrates got the reputation of being a wise man by going around trying to persuade people how little they knew. There is, of course, some truth in the ancient insight that awareness of ignorance is the beginning of wisdom. But it is just the beginning. We have to do something about it."

Good health,
Love,
Anna

I wrote this for you, Leona:

TREASURES

Treasures are kept inside usually,
Contained in a protected space.
Inside a friend, inside two minds.
Privacy between two minds.

Treasures are kept inside usually,
Wrapped, safe and secure
Inside a friend inside two minds.
Privacy between two minds.

Treasures are kept inside usually,
Taken out, admired and placed back
Inside a friend, inside two minds.
Privacy between two minds.

P.S. To know you is to wallow in wealth, treasured friend.

Love,
Anna

Letter To Sid

Dear Sid,

I was just thinking about you with loving thoughts of kindness while I was reading a note on happiness being a by-product of service — service being a law of our being.

It goes on to say, ". . . With love in our hearts, there is always service to our fellow man. A life of power, joy and satisfaction is built on love and service. A man who hates or is too selfish, is going against the love of his own being. He cuts himself off from God and his fellow man. Little acts of love and encouragement, of service and help, erase the rough spots of life and help to make the path smooth. If we do these things, we cannot help having our share of happiness . . ."

These beautiful thoughts I want to share with you because it reminds me of you. Thanks for your special acts of kindness. I hope we can share more of them.

I pray for your family's happiness and our frienship,

Love,
Anna

Letter To Andrea

Dear Andrea,

I really enjoy our time together. I'm thinking of a time when I knew a handsome tall young man. His love was like a living thing inside me. The sight of him could light my face, and fuel my heart for hours.

One evening while writing and listening to music, I thought about the "light" and wondered just how bright could it possibly glow. Does it take "him" to turn it on?

Out of all those thoughts came you, Andrea. I want to explore the birth and the death of that light. You are one of those rare, rare people who will sit with me and explore a thought — you can take one and give it light. It gets brighter still when two friends share it, doesn't it?

A note of thanks for being another light in my bright sky.

Love,
Anna

P.S. Emotions questioned become inclusive and illuminate; they want to add to our light. That's why they're so unhappy in the dark, I guess. (Anna)

Letter To Jack

Flowers from my garden to a man named Jack. If your work goes unnoticed, it will not be by me. I appreciate the effort you're making to preserve a little of America, the world and yourself. For any one of us who reads, writes, can see or feel the impact of the written word, you and people like you deserve a flower named for you. I'm delighted to hear about your new project in the paper industry.

You may be one of the best communicators of our time. Spoken or written, heard or voiced by you, there is a connection, a message, to and from a fine brain. A flower for your sight into our future, priceless friend.

Love,
Anna

A Note To George

Loving can be so paralyzing — In many ways more so than being unable to walk. I've experienced both and not walking is easier. With physical pain, there is a deadening and forgetting. The pain from love is not so easily forgotten — it reaches deep within, leaving all and nothing behind.

To George Gondron,
Love,
Anna

From Paulo, To Anna

A loved one
Trees, grass and a lake
A small house
With a fireplace:

Beethoven, Liszt or Chopin,
A cognac and a cigar.
Materialization of a dream,
or is it a dream of unreality?
Anyway, this is my dream.

Why fight a world that
I can't cope with?
Why join the forces that
Later on will kill me?
Competition? Society?
The insane and cruel murderers
Life?
The question beyond the question

Where is love?

The world I want
I can't reach it.
The woman I love
I can't have her.
My dream of a future
Is unreal

A loved one,
Trees
Grass and a lake
A small house
With a fireplace;

Beethoven, Liszt or Chopin,
A cognac and a cigar.
Materialization of a dream
Or is it a dream of
Unreality?
Anyway, it's just my life.

Love,
Paulo

To My Dear Husband

When I stop loving you
Will be,
When my body
They take away.
and —
The only sorrow you'll have
From me,
You will have had it,
On that day.

Love,
Anna

End of Saturday

I went inside to find the fire I'd built in the fireplace earlier in the day gradually going out. I watched the last red log turn white and the room got really cold. I'd had a Saturday of reading, writing and clay play. I was especially pleased with the clay piece I'd completed for Anna, a gift which I would present to her on our last day together.

Experiencing friendship value in a different way, I went to bed and pulled the heavy covers over me. A sad lonely feeling kept me from sleeping, the same feeling I'd experienced in the restaurant only a few nights ago.

I asked myself for the origin of that feeling, and a portrait of my ex-husband on a wall in an apartment in which we lived during the year 1965 appeared in my mind. The portrait was painted by Nolan Skipper in 1974. How weird! How could a portrait painted in 1974 appear on a 1965 wall? All I could think of was that those years were the beginning and the ending of the happiest years of my life. Nolan's portraits not only changed expressions, but changed body directions from every angle. When I couldn't communicate with my husband, I would look at his portrait and see the kindness in his eyes.

I forgot about sleeping and continued with the reframe of that feeling of sadness. The sadness began to turn into deep hurt and the pain of being unable to talk to someone.

That someone became my mother almost immediately. My word! The years of feeling hurt because I couldn't get her attention — then she died. I projected that childhood pain onto my husband and pouted when he wouldn't listen to me.

Reframing my past using this technique was interesting. I decided to be in control of that part of my past as Anna and I had discussed. I created an image of my mother, my ex-husband and me having a discussion. I told them what I needed. The feeling changed from hurt to love almost immediately.

The last thing I remember before going to sleep was smiling and thinking, "What do you do when you can't sleep? Change your ex-husband, of course!"

Sunday

The following morning was cold and foggy. It was Sunday and I wouldn't be going to Anna's house. I expected a visit from Gail, who had a weekend place nearby. I started my car and remembered that I'd not driven more than a few blocks in weeks except for short trips to the grocery store every now and then. My days were Anna, home, homework, sleep, meditation, food, writing and walking. I went to the bird sanctuary and later to the chapel for meditation.

I thought about the reframe of my sadness the night before and what I'd learned from it. The message is that I can now think of my ex-husband and my mother as people and friends and take them out of their traditionally confined roles.

Gail came for lunch. She said it was impossible to spend that much time with Anna. She was convinced I'd found a lover I didn't want her to know about. Gail saw all the paper around the typewriter. "See, I knew it. You're having some clandestine romance and writing about it. You'll probably publish it under another name, and I'll never know what I witnessed."

In many ways she was right, except that it was a loving story. I loved Anna, I loved my time alone, I loved getting to know Laura through her writings. I loved my lessons. I loved

what I was writing each night. My writing was all too fresh
and private to share at that time. When I told Gail how much
I valued her friendship, she wanted to know if the sea gulls
were bringing me messages from afar.

"You have changed! What's happening? I love it, whatever
it is."

We promised to see each other at our group's Christmas
party. I reread some of Anna's letters before I went to sleep.

CHAPTER

TEN

Monday, December 20, 1982

"Waffles with fresh whipped butter, crisp bacon, cane syrup, a large glass of cold milk and French roast coffee" were the first words I heard from Anna. "This cold day is perfect for a heavy breakfast. It's perfect for the bulbs, and it's also perfect for reviewing what you and I have planted.

"I think all days are perfect! Each morning I'm thrilled to wake up to all the surprises. Let's cook while you tell me about friendships. Did you learn anything?"

"Anna, I learned that the most valuable therapy can only be found in a friend and that it's probably the most expensive, demanding and rewarding of all therapy. To be and keep a friend takes a natural therapist and a competent gardener. A friend must be an artist of giving, receiving and discarding. To be and keep a friend, we must have very sensitive communication skills and be flexible with our time, tolerance and talent. And yet there is still something missing." I emphasized the "something missing" part. "I guess that explains why we have so few friends. What an

93

awesome responsibility to be asked to become your new best friend, Anna."

"And what is that 'something missing?' " she wanted to know.

"Maybe something I wrote to you yesterday will explain it."

To Anna, From Zoe:

I know a friend when I see one,
There's a special look.
Or hear one, there's a special sound.
To feel the lack of tension, there's a special feeling.
It takes two to be a friend,
One to give and one to receive.
Like magic, these roles friends exchange.
Still, there's always something missing.
A SCOREKEEPER!

She told me where to put it in her notebook and how pleased she felt. I was not so pleased with the awareness of the responsibility of a friendship. I tried to explain all this to Anna and she shushed me, saying, "Be responsible 'to' but not 'for' your friends and loved ones."

The Curb Of Knowledge

By mid-morning the weather had warmed to a moist, low cloud. Anna took every opportunity to be outside. I felt sticky and lifeless and couldn't breathe while she seemed to thrive on it. She pulled weeds and dragged water hoses all over the place. I have no idea how she knew where to place the things. She just did it. She joined me at my favorite sitting spot on her "curb of knowledge."

Anna's Ob-Coms

Today, she wanted me to know the difference between an obsession and a compulsion, which she called "Ob-Coms."

She explained, "I know you and your group have studied this subject until you have lost the true working meaning of it. All of us use the words, but I think there's a definite need to know the difference. Most people think about irrational acts and anxiety disorders when they talk about obsessions and compulsions. Save that for your group. I want to talk about good and bad 'ob-coms.'

"Obsessions are repeated thoughts about the same thing. It's strictly a mind thing. A compulsion is acting on those thoughts.

"I've learned to go with mine. They usually last about six months. I struggled like Brer Rabbit and Tar Baby for years with my ob-coms. The more I fought one, the more stuck I got. I eventually learned to go with them. If I became obsessed with a subject, I would exclude all areas of my life until I'd exhaust myself with the subject, experience burn-out and never want a thing to do with the subject again. I give myself total permission to enjoy them now, those good for me.

"I know that my energy for any subject is short lived, but during that time I will gain massive amounts of information. The secret is not to exclude my friends and family or deny myself other needs, and I know that's near impossible.

"Another thing I know for sure is that nothing was ever accomplished or will ever be completed without a degree of ob-com. I'm protective of mine, can you tell?

Kahlil Gibran

"Kahlil Gibran said, 'Compulsion is a mirror in which he who looks for long will see the inner self endeavoring to commit suicide.'

"You can be sure he was talking about compulsions that are bad for us. I'd like to thank Kahlil for his words and keep looking behind the mirror, behind the compulsion, back to the obsession, back to the thoughts we have before we act out the thoughts — back to something about which we have choice. From there we can look further back to what's lurking in the shadows.

"I agree with Laura that three good indicators of addiction are compulsion, loss of control and continued use of our drug of choice, in spite of adverse consequences.

Obsessions

"When we think about our drug of choice, whether it be our loved ones, smoking, food, sex, booze, drugs, abusive people, working to excess, overspending, excesses of all kinds like house-cleaning, car-cleaning, washing hands, pacing, perfecting all our loved ones, or whatever we know is bad for us that we continue to do. When we think repeated thoughts about it, that's the obsession. What do we think about all the time and do nothing to correct? That's my point today. Stick with me!

Compulsions

"Listen now, Miss Zoe. When we reach out for it, complete the act, ingest the substance or take the abuse one more time, that's the compulsion. So take a look at what you are doing; that's important.

"I want to talk about the importance of separating the obsession and the compulsion and the precious little time between them. During that split little bit of time, we'd better do something; or we'll do the same old thing we've always done.

"Some lives are lived around an obsession, planning it into one's life and justifying it to one's self. What's funny and sad is convincing someone else that you have to have your drug of choice. And what's funnier and sadder than that is watching that someone help you do it.

Addict-Additions

"Can we agree that anything that controls us against our better judgment is an addiction?

"Addictions are everywhere, including addict-additions.

"Notice, I said additions, something added. I like to make up words," Anna laughed at herself. "Translated, that means someone who depends on a dependent person. An addict is dependent on what he is addicted to and if we are controlled in any way by his drug of choice, then aren't we addicted to the addict? Aren't we out of control against our better judgment?

"Sounds like scrambled eggs to me. That's one reason separate yolks are so important. We kill each other off if we don't separate our yolks.

"Common ob-coms are things you can see with your eyes or feel with your hands, taste with your mouth or smell with your nose. Let's go further into you," Anna said.

I wasn't sure I wanted to hear this, but little did she care. She told me my problem was being obsessed with my problems — how I keep going back to my problems the same as a chemical abuser goes back to the chemical. Her advice was to substitute the name of the person or my problem in the place of the chemical.

Phone Ob-Coms

"Let's pretend that you are obsessed with your friend, Stan, and that it's hard for you to understand that a phone call made by you to him is the same as a beer to an alcoholic. You think about him, you rationalize a phone call to him, you re-feel all those old feelings, you continue to think about him, you reach for the phone, you pick up the phone, you dial the phone. If contact is made with him, you complete the cycle. If not, you "obsess" about him. Where is he? You build it larger and larger. You must reach him! You are well into your ob-com phone number, and you can't be stopped. This behavior continues until you get what you have to have. When you get the feeling you need — and the feeling can be awful or wonderful or any number of other responses — that's when you stop.

"When do you have the power to replace this obsession with something more powerful than the response you know you will experience from reaching this person? When?

"To take the time to observe how you keep the addiction active takes a little insight. Remember, a phone call made by you to him is the same as a beer to an alcoholic.

"You may have to have one more. If so, there is nothing I can do for you. Just like the alcoholic when he forgets why he quit, he starts again. So will you if you forget why the telephone call is bad for you.

"Do you think you can out-think an addiction? You can't. Don't try. That's a good way to die. This is a time to do something. Act! That's the only magic. Action — do something other than what you've been doing.

"If you can do something other than reach out for your poison — your phone — one time, there's a pretty good chance you can repeat the positive action. Keep this up as long as it is difficult to do. Don't ask questions, don't let your negative mind have a chance to over-rule your action. Don't think about it. Do something. If you take time to think about it, the chances increase that you'll do it." Anna couldn't be stopped. Words kept flowing.

Wisdom To Know The Difference

"Wisdom is when you act on your knowledge and become wise enough to let go — that rare moment when you no longer talk about something, when you no longer have the need to hear yourself say the same old thing over and over to impress your audience with your knowledge. You wisely listen to others go through the same old worn-out struggle that took you so long. Not wise with pride, not wising off about how you did it, just the awareness of how you once struggled with the same thing. Wisdom is happy that it needs to learn no more about a specific struggle."

Letting Go Workshops

I interrupted. "Anna, I've been in letting go programs forever. I think I'll start some letting go workshops and have everyone act out all your examples. Before I do that, though, I need some help on something."

I told her about my re-frame of my ex-husband and mother, and then I said, "I miss my ex-husband and parts of our marriage, but I know we can't live together. I had a lot of energy locked into a one-and-only marriage that I was determined to make work. Maybe I didn't try long or hard enough. I know that kind of reasoning is nonsense, but I want to acknowledge that it still exists so I can go on beyond that feeling of failure."

"Here you go with the 'buts' '. . . but I'm different,' '. . . but, . . . but . . . but.' If you're in conflict, you are still holding on to something. Until you let go and allow yourself to be out of control for a while, you'll stay in conflict.

"Read the crab stories over and over." Her voice changed from corrective to consoling.

"For instance, a friend of mine wrote a letter many years ago to a man she loved very much.

"Let's go inside and you can read it to me.

"She had to swim on ahead of him. He got caught up in his alcoholism. The lady who wrote it knew not to argue with an addiction, the same as I knew to swim ahead of my best friend. You, too, Lady Zoe, are swimming on ahead. Maybe he will make it and maybe not. The important thing for you is that you have to keep swimming or both of you will drown. Together you were sinking, is that what you're saying?

"Enjoy this beer, little tree, we're going inside to learn about folks who can't drink half a beer," she said, as she emptied the can of beer onto a huge and leaf-bare, light purple Althea tree. She'd planted it when it had been only a twig, about ten years earlier. Every plant in her yard had a history and she made sure I recognized each of them by name, color and age, bare and bearing.

"When I say wives of alcoholics, I know that women can also be alcoholics. I just can't think fast enough to say he and she. You can rearrange all that."

Anna rambled on. "If he could control it, he wouldn't be an alcoholic. That's what a non-alcoholic usually can't understand. He may know it's killing him, but he drinks in spite of this knowledge. Now you figure that one out. One drink is too much and all the drinks in the world are not enough. Another thing the non-alcoholic can't understand is that his decision to drink has very little to do with her.

"Look in the notebook under *Letting go of Ob-Coms*. You should find a letter written to Karl. Listen as you read. He had already found a sure cure for himself, and the writer knew she had nothing more powerful to offer him. So she let go."

Letter To Karl

Dearest Karl,

I've observed your self-consciousness. I've heard your doubts. I've felt your fears. I, too, fear for you the dreaded disease of alcoholism. I've watched you have a drink to cover your self-consciousness. You take a drink and then the drink takes you. The drink makes you think you are confident. If a chemical has the power to change your self-image, be aware of its power.

To be painfully self-conscious is miniscule compared to the theft of all your self-respect. In time there is nothing you have that alcoholism won't take. You will build a natural tolerance to the alcohol, and it will take more of the same chemical to give you relief.

Meanwhile the self-consciousness has grown. You've been robbed of all the growth you could have been experiencing from dealing with the pain of your self-consciousness.

Dreams are Mother Nature's therapy and alcohol causes you to have bizarre dreams or none at all. Without her therapy the sieves between your conscious and unconscious will get clogged. Your thinking will get distorted, and the drink will become essential. Your body will become dependent on alcohol. In time, everything gets out of proportion — small things get larger and the large things will get smaller.

The judgment and reasoning you once used to make decisions, now find justification in more and more alcohol. The loud songs you sing take on new words and new meaning — what a friend you've found in alcohol. Keep bringing in the wheat and corn and the old rugged cross gets harder to carry.

Loving and accepting the self-consciousness and dealing with it sounds simple now, doesn't it? Think of a child learning to walk; how clumsy it first appears. To one who knows how many falls and how much determination it takes to walk, this can be viewed with admiration and love. I feel the same love toward the ups and downs of recovery. I want everything for you, Karl. I know that what I want for you is not enough — you must want it. You must be willing to go through the pain. I can't do that for you.

Betty D.

P.S. You can't kill yourself without my love, but you'll have to kill yourself without my help. Good luck!

End of Ninth day with Anna

Anna sent me home. She said I'd had enough insight for one day. That evening I didn't make a phone call, that's for sure. I didn't plan ahead to have lunch with a friend of my ex-husband or read old letters that I had brought along to read just once again before I threw them away or go through business papers that just couldn't wait another day or any of the old ways that kept me from moving on.

". . . Knowledge is proud that he has learned so much." Those words were going over and over in my mind obsessively, waiting to be acted on. I began a lengthy meditation, consciously repeating a prayer to give me wisdom to know what I needed to know.

After that day and that meditation I let go of the feeling of failure and the yearning about which I had talked with Anna. The worry that I could have done a better job of marriage or stayed longer became vapor. It now felt like a loving decision full of memories — good and bad — but mostly it felt like experience and a very solid stepping stone into the future. The sadness, the reframe, the talking with Anna about the feeling, the meditation and prayer reminded me of a good twelve-step solution to absolution.

CHAPTER
ELEVEN

Tuesday, December 21, 1982

Anna was in bed when I arrived.

"I'm a little lazy lady this morning. You'd think I didn't have a thing to do the way I'm carrying on. I've been lying here half awake, and I have no idea where the other half is — it's not awake. Many years ago I decided that if I wake up, I get up!"

It seemed only natural to put my hands on her shoulders and gently lift her. She looked so fragile. But I was in for the lecture of my life.

"I'm no invalid and I won't be treated as one. Help me with your love, and you'll kill me with your love. Wait until I ask you to help me. Don't think that you know what I want. Believe me, I ask for what I need."

Anna watched my awkward response for an uncomfortable period of time before she began to smile.

Detachment

"That lesson should keep your little rescuing neurons firing off on 'detachment' all day. I plan drama into my lessons to stimulate all your memory senses. I promised you a lengthy lesson on Wives of Alcoholics someday, and today is the day. Do you have any questions?"

"I'll make myself some coffee while you dress yourself, Anna. Is the other half of you awake? If so, tell it I got your message and that I'm ready to practice."

"Today's message is not so easily learned. I wish it were, Miss Zoe. I want you to practice not doing one thing for anyone today unless you're asked! That's gonna mess you up for a little while.

"Being gracious and generous as you and I were taught has to be untaught. I'm not asking you to do it forever. I want you to have a choice. If you can't do what I'm asking for one day, you sure won't get today's lesson!

"Remember, I'm asking you to do it 'just for today.' If there's value in it for you, you can do it 'just for yourself' in the future."

I made coffee, cooked one poached egg and one slice of dry toast, peeled one orange, poured one glass of milk, and put one place mat on the table with one teaspoon, one fork, one knife and one napkin. I had just sat down when she came into the room.

The discipline of not moving one muscle to help her was unfamiliar. I'd been dashing ahead of her trying to make life a little easier. I'd only wanted to help, I reasoned, as I watched her trying to find things. Then I saw it — it was so obvious — she was becoming dependent on me. Anna had survived by not allowing herself to become dependent.

Her breakfast of heavy cream, dry cereal and buttered toast didn't appeal to me at all. She said, "See what you'd be eating if you were nice. Saying 'no' to future plans is not the only 'no' you must learn. Learn to say 'no' to certain foods or change it. I know you don't want my rich diet, but you keep eating it day after day."

"Anna, Anna, Anna, you precious, dear, dear lady! You may very well be the best of the best teachers. There's no end to your lessons, is there?"

"What I've been able to give to you will determine that. If you're ready to receive more of what's been given to me, we'll go for it."

Wives Of Alcoholics

Anna began, "I want to keep it simple today so I'll start by saying that people marry people, and people become alcoholics. I want to say right up front that any sober alcoholic has clearly defined boundaries or he couldn't stay sober. He has more knowledge of recovery and scrambled eggs than most people writing or talking about them, including me.

"I think of alcoholism like I think of pregnancy. Anyone can diagnose pregnancy in the eighth month. It takes someone who knows about pregnancy to diagnose it in the first month.

"It doesn't take much education to diagnose alcoholism in its final stages either. Earlier on, it's a different story. If you've got alcoholism, you'll carry it full term. If you've got it, you'll be an alcoholic, drunk or sober, until you die. Unlike pregnancy there is no aborting alcoholism.

"Alcoholics can be so lovable that we just love them to death. We try to buy, deny or do what the alcoholic must do for himself.

"A smart wife who is dealing with active alcoholism goes to Cling Clinic Meetings for families. If she learns the art of letting go, she'll get out of the way. She'll turn his alcoholism over to the only one who can do something about it — him. She'll consult qualified professionals and follow directions.

"She'll take care of herself and leave him free to get well or get worse. (She'll cook her own egg and let him sip on his own cream.) She'll let go!

" 'Letting go' doesn't mean leaving her home, it doesn't mean hating him and it doesn't mean giving up.

"It means no more excuses, no more abuse, no more denial, no more blaming, no more accusing, no more teaching or controlling him in any way. A woman who can do all that has learned all the crab stories. She knows how to let go.

"Remember my lesson this morning on waiting to be asked before you do something for me. That's one way to begin to get unscrambled. Just stop doing whatever you are

doing for someone. Watch everyone readjust. Or ask
someone to stop doing something and mean it. Remember
your reaction?"

"Certainly I remember. You could cure Alzheimer himself
with that example!" I reacted.

Anna said, "I'll see it when I believe it. That's another way
of saying 'Do it first, then look at it.' Do you understand the
importance of that?"

"I'm ready to hear more."

"No woman I've known ever married her husband because
he was alcoholic, and she doesn't divorce him because he's
alcoholic. The hope that the alcoholic will return to loving
her obsessively as he once did allows no other to compete
with that memory or fade that hope.

Gates Of Insanity

"There's always the wife who rides this thing through the
gates of insanity to death, just as some alcoholics do but that's
no reason to brand everyone who ever married an alcoholic
with the same disorder."

"Anna, my dad once said, 'If a bull frog jumps into a tub of
heating water, he'll stay in the water until he boils to death.
But, if he jumps into a tub of boiling water, he'll jump out
immediately.' "

Anna said . . . "Now that just about tells it all. We could
end the lecture there, but, we won't. There's always the
question, 'Who turned up the burner?' "

"It can get hot fast in an alcoholic home. Let's say the water
in this tub is getting plenty uncomfortable. The old boy gets
drunk, and the wife releases her frustrations all over
everything and everybody.

"The outcome is that she now has more guilt from the
hatred expressed, and the alcoholic makes more promises.
The alcoholic's promises, although rarely kept, keep her
hope alive. They forgive each other again.

"The troubled little boy she finds in her bed in the
morning wins her heart over and over. They both know

where and when to say the right and wrong words, and the marriage-go-round goes round after round.

"Treatment, the modern hope of all hopes, interrupted so often by another drinking bout, does little to make or break this marriage because this wife just goes deeper into what she has done for so long. She can't leave and she can't stay. She feels crazy and more insecure.

"She becomes afraid to make a decision — the only person she has in her life who still believes her is her drunk husband. He believes she will scream, curse him and throw him out, as he thinks he deserves. He also believes she will take him back again, as she thinks she deserves.

"They are now locked into the same downward spiral, and all they have is each other. They have to have each other to live. He has to have what's killing him to stay alive — alcohol. She has no self-esteem, no yolk. She's now scrambled and she has to have what's killing her to survive — him.

"I want you to read a letter that Laura wrote to the *Houston Chronicle*. She never mailed it because they were asking what could be done about drug abuse, and Laura didn't think she answered the question. She sent it to me as a writing homework assignment instead."

Houston Chronicle

I just read your editorial and the question, "Is Drug Abuse Threatening America's Bright Future And What Would I Do About It?"

I have been reviewing the past 50 years of my life in relationship to drugs and alcohol and their far-reaching effects: the broken dreams of the abuser and the permanent emotional damage to all of us for many generations to come.

I began volunteering in the alcoholism and drug-abuse field in 1965 after knowing that my husband's drinking was different from mine. Trying to find the answers for him, I found some for me. But tragically information was limited. My dear precious ex-husband, now dying from the side effects of this dreaded disease, had an alcoholic father and brother. Our daughter, 19 years old, died in an automobile accident — the result of her own budding alcoholism.

His father had attempted recovery numerous times, beginning in 1934. His children and the children's children are still suffering.

Most recently, the 21-year-old son of my husband's brother died in a motorcycle accident — again alcohol and drug-related.

My family has the same story: an alcoholic father with several children abusing alcohol. The disease continues into the grandchildren.

I ask as you have, "How can we stop a legal or an illegal substance from entering the systems of our people?"

I work in an alcoholism and drug-abuse rehabilitation center as a counselor. Burn-out among the professionals is so very common. And I, too, often wonder if I should not move on. However, when a family member calls me, I can't not share my experience, strength and hope. I pray for help for the entire family, all the while knowing that we are losing the fight — yes, losing!

In the treatment centers we try to rehabilitate a person after many years of abuse. Change behavior in 28 days? Most of us know the percentage of lifetime dedication to recovery after 28 days, but any percentage is more than a few short years ago.

Then, too, the wives. For years most of us have tried to keep our families together.

We've had our homes and our families bombed, and we were the only ones who knew there was a war. Then comes the memory of what we didn't do and what we could have done. We forget to remember our own pain at the time we were frantically searching for answers. We knew there was an answer because someone else found it. We heard about "letting go" and we tried to let go until the next person asked, ". . . but have you tried *so and so* . . . ?" and So and So won again.

Oh, God, and then it's our children . . . and it almost always is. Rarely is there time for us to recover from one war before another is to be fought.

When we have to stop, we feel guilty for not having done everything. We then have another wasted life, just as wasted as the alcoholic's life. We feel like failures. We feel that alcohol has cost us our lives as well as his.

When I saw your question, I saw a picture.

A picture of Americans circling America for relief of pain. Our own large circle of people protection. A circle to protect our shores and our airways from drugs. Each state circling each state and each county circling each county and each community circling each community and each neighborhood circling each neighborhood until our own love becomes the cure. A drug-free society. Only a dream!

I warn you not to get too educated. You'll know how most people treat their psychological disorders. They treat their own phobias and depressions with drugs and alcohol. What will replace all this insanity? What will calm the fears? Are we willing to look?

Laura

"There's not a lot of hope in that letter," Anna commented. "But is it the truth? I think the help that is available today is marvelous. Laura, my competent little therapist friend, sees too much abuse. She gets burned out with the reality of it all."

"Anna, if you had written a letter, what would you have said? What can be done?" I asked.

"Questions, questions, questions, that's all I hear. And I, too, only have questions. I can't help you much here. I don't know how willing we are to take a look at what drugs and alcohol are doing for us. Notice, I said 'for' us not 'to' us.

"Let's assume that all eyes, ears and minds are open. Where would we start? Do we have the facilities, the institutions, the hospitals and professionals to care for the mental illness that drugs and alcohol are keeping under check until the drugs and alcohol kill our loved ones?

"Drugs and alcohol do kill pain — emotional and physical pain. Can we deal with that pain if we take the pain killers off the market? Has the pain accelerated with each new generation until alcohol no longer can meet the needs of our young people?

"How much more pressure can our young ones take?

"How much pain do they inherit?

"How much faster can they go?

"How many more baskets can they shoot?

"How much more sex do they need?

"Like I said, I can't help much. All I have are questions. My question remains constant. What are drugs and alcohol doing 'for' us, not 'to' us?"

"I, too, only have questions. Our eggs are so scrambled, I'm not sure where the common boundary is anymore. Now don't let me depress you. There's more help for those asking for help today than there has ever been, and more professionals are agreeing on treatment than ever before.

"Don't let anyone convince you he wasn't drunk or abusive to you. If you saw him drunk, he was drunk. Keeping your yolk separate can be just about that difficult. If someone other than you can convince you that what you saw, felt or heard was not true, then your little yolk is in grave trouble. Keep your little yolk separate, regardless of who you marry. That's my advice to the world."

Anna quit talking and I stared at her. During that silence my mind wandered to frogs, scrambled eggs and soft-shelled crabs. I began to be thankful and grateful, and I knew that I had to give it away to keep it.

I said, "I have an urge to write. In fact, I have to write!"

I went to the room with all the books, closed the door and I started typing.

December 21, 1982

I heard the basic story of the following from my dad when I was eight years old while he and I were fishing.

Fisherman

Fisherman got up early each morning, eager to spend some of his leisure time doing what he enjoyed doing most — fishing. He gave fish to neighbors, friends and strangers and became known as Fisherman.

After catching all the fish he and his loved ones could eat that day, he happily went home to spend time with his wife and children. They gardened and did chores together while he related most of life's experiences to fishing and nature.

Fisherman taught financial planning with simple stories about the importance of leaving the small fish to grow.

When he was asked why there were problems and disharmony in the world, he associated troubles with the sharp fins that have been put on some fish to keep all the other fish stirring — to keep them from getting too fat and dying young.

The word 'value' was always attached to words like honesty and respect for others. 'Compensation' was what one received from obeying the laws of the community.

The children were taught the consequences of disobeying the laws of gravity and authority.

Fish stories were substituted for fairy tales in Fisherman's home.

The children and wife of Fisherman were always content and full of love. They shared their stories just as Fisherman did his catch each day.

People from distant places came to their happy home to be blessed with their continuing good fortune.

One day a very wealthy businessman approached Fisherman and asked him to sell his fish for a profit.

Fisherman asked the businessman what he would do with the money.

The businessman told him he could buy a larger boat. Fisherman wanted to know why he needed a larger boat from the one he and his children had built.

The businessman told him he could catch and store more fish for sale. He could buy a whole fleet of boats and make even more money.

Fisherman wanted to know what he would do when he had all that money.

The businessman said, "You could then have time to fish and be with your family."

Fisherman understood the logic of the businessman, but the businessman could only hear himself and wanted to argue his point.

Fisherman became very quiet, baited his hook, shook his head in disbelief, squinted his eyes with love and tolerance for the businessman.

Fisherman gently refused the offer by saying, "I thought that was what I was doing."

When I had a problem, my dad took me fishing and told me fish stories. I named him Fisherman. I remember more of his lessons; but I had other educators and I learned from them as well.

Pleasure

Whoever planned this life for all of us gave it to us one day at a time without the answers. We have to find the question to find the answers. An exciting puzzle, don't you think?

Wouldn't it be dull if we were only here to procreate? Wasn't it smart of whoever planned it all to install a little pleasure center in the brain right along with the neurons that fire off saying, "Okay, it's time to make another baby?" And in that same little center of the brain that smart maker of us connected pleasure with hunger and thirst as well as sex.

We go madly in search of satisfying these basic needs, not because we are so concerned about the future — future generations — but in search of pleasure.

Pleasure Abuse

Some people have abused the brain with chemicals that go across the delicate pleasure area of the brain like fingernail polish remover goes through lacquer on a fine finished table.

The chemicals cause the pleasure neurons to fire off more frequently than Mother Nature intended. And forever after, the abuser's neurons will fire erratically with or without the chemicals.

After being over-stimulated, the pleasure circuits shut down and leave only pain and craving — for food, thirst and sex. What remains is every possible combination of compulsive disorders. The abuser or ex-abuser will forever be in quest of something to turn that little center of pleasure on or off again — something to put the little pleasure center back in charge — back in control of what was once taken for granted, what was once enjoyed and of what we all want more: *pleasure.*

Fisherman's stories are too, too simple for most of us. If we could only have the good judgment of Fisherman and have the courage to have less, maybe we would find that by having less we have more.

Retirement

If I am the young person who will be caring for the old person I am to become, I want to accumulate more fish and crab stories, I want to know more egg theories and I want to have someone to whom I can will my good fortune. (Zoe, 1982)

I stopped writing and walked around the book room, thinking about Cowper's words and my detour from the gates of insanity: ". . . Knowledge is proud that he has learned so much." I was feeling sad and glad — sad that it had been necessary for me to have learned as much as I'd learned about alcoholism and drugs, but so very, very grateful that I'd learned no more. ". . . Wisdom is humble that he knows no more . . ."

I joined Anna in the kitchen. She made hot tea while I read to her what I'd written. Her influence was becoming more evident in everything I wrote and she knew it.

When I stopped reading, I looked at her. She had "that look" — the one she had just before she made one of her concise remarks. "Story-telling will get you a long way in this world. I'm honored to commingle my fortune with Fisherman's. However, you know inheritance is a tremendous responsibility — distribution can be a problem."

Anna changed the subject to inform me that we would be driving to a nearby city the following day. She wanted to deliver her own Christmas gifts.

"Anna, you know day after tomorrow will be my last day with you, don't you?" I reminded her. "I must get back before Christmas, remember?"

Anna refused to acknowledge that I would be leaving. She said, "You'll want to wear a pair of blue jeans."

End of Tenth Day with Anna

I went Christmas shopping and decided that Santa was here to stay. I learned on my seventh birthday to quit expecting people to remember a Christmas birthday. If I wanted something, I bought it for myself. This year, I couldn't think of a thing I wanted. Anna had been my gift.

CHAPTER
TWELVE

Wednesday, December 22, 1982

Anna was dressed in naturally faded blue jeans and a plaid shirt. She gave me a handwritten page of directions to Lisa's and Darrell's home. We put the gifts and her bag into the back seat of the car, and we began our 30-mile journey.

"Look again at the trees while we drive," Anna said. "They're still together, and they are certainly close. I don't believe they withstood the hurricanes by clinging to each other, do you? They each had their own root system, their own supply of sunshine and drew from those sources, not always from each other."

Commitment

Anna taught all the way, "I want to talk about commitment. That word is singular to me. 'Borne in my knowledge of the word and reared in my wisdom.' " She quoted an expression of her mother's. "I can't know what commitment means to another person if I live with them forever.

"One person — me only — making a commitment is important. Living up to the commitment gives me freedom.

To impinge on that trust destroys something within me. My commitment has nothing to do with the other person. This belief relieves me of the lifetime concern for another's fidelity, leaving me with abundant energy to build, create and learn.

"With freedom and knowledge, I can become more committed to long range goals, and people can trust my word. Other people can make their own commitment. I have nothing to do with their part.

"I trust the space between you and me, and I love every close second of it.

"Another thing I want to say is that I am patient now. That's one thing worth developing — patience. I decided a long time ago that if I didn't develop patience, I would become one."

Crabby Attitudes

Anna continued. "I've learned that by letting go, being willing to change and looking ahead, I can change a lifetime of old attitudes in a short time. I know this by the way I have adjusted to other changes. I'm usually willing to let go all the way to the tiny fingers of my 'crabby attitudes.' Sometimes I need someone to hold a mirror for me so I can see the attitudes that are so old, they have barnacles all over them. But by and large, I stay ready and open for change.

"All one has to say is, 'Let go, Anna.' You can be sure when I hear those words, I listen. You know, I get excited talking about this. Do you want me to continue?" she asked.

Comfort

"I'd like to be certain of who to plant and who to weed out. You seem to know, Anna. How can you be so certain?" I asked.

"That's easy. I love comfort. I love balance. I feel balance. When my inside and outside pressure is right, I know it." Anna spoke with confidence.

"I'm no longer a victim of the elements. I have a home out of the wind and weather. I can change the air conditioning to any temperature I want. I've worked for that luxury, just as I've worked to know with whom I'm comfortable. Why should I be a victim to my feelings? I don't need a thermostat to tell me if I feel comfort or balance. If I weed out all the people with whom I feel emotion, I'll be alone. Is that what you are getting ready to say?"

I quit answering her questions. I knew they were part of her teaching.

Immunity To Pain

"Your question was, how do I know who to weed out? Well, I know that you are a splendid mirror for me. I don't need sight for that. I do need some intelligence to know that if I like something about you enough that my emotions are stirred up, I already possess what I like about you. If I dislike something about you with a lot of emotion, I can claim that also and learn whatever I need to know about me. If I'm wise, I'll correct it.

"It's like getting an immunity shot to protect me from chicken pox. If I claim what I like or dislike about you and accept or correct it about myself, it may hurt for a short while but then I'm immune. Otherwise I'm a victim over and over. And I catch the feeling every time someone similar is nearby.

"If I let my emotions run my life and weed out all the people around me with whom I feel extreme emotion, we all lose and indeed I will be very lonely.

"That was an unplanned lesson on projections. Projections are always at an unconscious level. They are some of the best yolk builders you'll find. Few of us are fortunate enough to recognize our projections and learn from them, but they are worth every minute of time you invest. The very best place to start learning about your own projections is to observe your emotional reaction to someone. If you have a lot of emotion, you need to isolate that moment in time and ask yourself a few questions. What does that person represent to me that I've not accepted about me? Life will become easier fast when you start doing that for yourself. I

know you know a lot about projections from Carl Jung and
Irene Corbit, art therapist; now you can add 'Anna, Chapter
1: Verse 4.'

Pincher Sharpeners

"Write some every day; that's the best way I know to keep
your garden weeded and your pinchers sharp." She laughed.
"You can write anything into a story. You can put your
greatest fantasy into a story and know the outcome,
experience it and decide if that's what you want. That's what
I do. Writing frees the feet of one's mind, I believe.

"Of course, there will be people who want to hold you to
every word you write. I don't think you're infallible, so how
can what you write be infallible? To think a thing is so today
because it was so yesterday? How boring! No art of discard
in that way of thinking. No letting go, no room for new birth.
But do acknowledge your errors and limitations quickly to
free those little feet so they can keep searching.

"Above all, trust people. Why not? I trust me, so I trust that
you won't harm me any more than I will harm you. I'm
taking advantage of you this minute. You're filling my need
to give what I have received. You are some of the best eyes
I've ever had and I feel protected in your presence."

I looked at the water as we drove along the coast, just
feeling and thinking. Most of all, I didn't want to interrupt
her thinking.

Anna continued, "I think the insight of most people today
is a miracle of the times. The help and research is beyond
anything my mind can comprehend. A problem I see is that
you don't know what to do with it all. Quite often, it's so
simple you folks miss it."

At Home Atmosphere

Anna, now emphatic. "Something simple to know that has
helped me is that we all grew up with an atmosphere in our
homes — good or bad, intense or calm. We all had a familiar
atmosphere. Hated or loved — our atmosphere became
familiar. We spend the remainder of our lives recreating that

'at home atmosphere', whether we liked it or not. I'd go so far as to say that we will go to any length to recreate that feeling.

"Just like a compass, looking for the opposite puts me in the same spot at another place with another person. From there I have only questions. How powerful are our thoughts? How much influence do we have over another person with our thoughts?"

Anna, now more emphatic, talked on. "Go back to what you said about resentments, resentir and re-feeling. Isolating feelings are not simple. I think the feeling we are left with, like the garbage after a feast, is the pay-off, don't you? That's the 'at home atmosphere,' the one we keep recreating.

"Yes, I do indeed think all the help that's available today is valuable, if it helps you to stop a few minutes in time and think about 'that familiar feeling.' Any help that assists you in isolating your 'at home feeling' and teaches you how you keep recreating it can be most beneficial, I believe."

Lisa's And Darrell's

The directions were accurate. Our day with Darrell and Lisa was more interesting than I'd expected. They were young and intelligent. I didn't expect Anna to give me background on anyone I met through her because she wanted me to have my own experience.

The four of us went to the shrimp boats and visited Anna's other friends. Lisa and I decided to stay behind while they went from one boat to another. We sat on the back of one shrimp boat and talked about living in a small town, the advantages and disadvantages. We experienced our boat, securely tied to the dock, reacting to the other boat's wake. Lisa's keen mind reacted just as accurately. "When my husband does the least little thing that reminds me of his behavior while he was drinking and drugging, I react just like this boat is reacting. I feel tied and anchored. I sit in place and I let everything he does control me."

Anna's words drifted across my mind: "I have to give it away to keep it; everyone knows that. Pass it on. You'll know to whom."

"If you're reacting to his wake, you haven't learned the art of letting go," I heard myself saying with absolute certainty. "Letting go is an art. If you want to be the happiest person you can possibly be, you must perfect the art of letting go."

After telling Lisa about Anna's letter to Virginia and how a Gulf Crab grows, I said, "Reacting to his wake can become your conscious awareness that you are swimming in his waters. If you don't get out of his waters, you'll adjust to that uncertainty and you'll both lose your individuality."

Lisa and I decided that the boat had no choice but to react. We have a choice. Lisa questioned about letting go of her fear to love and trust her husband again. We forgot about the boat and the time of day as we exchanged one experience after another.

Anna's Gift From The Gulf

In the early afternoon Anna said, "Before we leave this island, I want some private time with you, Miss Zoe. Let's drive to the beach. I have something I want to hear you read before it gets too late."

After lengthy good-byes with Lisa and Darrell, Anna gave specific directions to one of her favorite places on the beach front. The day was cloudy and turning cold. Anna wanted to be quiet for a little while. She meditated while I looked across the water into whiteness.

The beach in the winter has a desolate emptiness for me. The sound of the waves brings and takes surging sadness until some car noise or the sight of a sea gull reminds me of other sensations.

Anna gently said, "It's my latest dictation, my Christmas present to you. My daughter typed it last night. It's all for you, from me with love." Anna gave me an envelope tied with a tiny yellow ribbon. Inside was a typed letter to Lady Zoe.

Cling Clinics

Cling Clinics are everywhere, Lady Zoe.
Some crabs lead you to the mud for your transformation;

others help you while you're in the mud and others lead you out of the mud. Some crabs swim right along with you.

Notice that the big free beautiful ones go back to the mud often, sharing freely with other crabs. Notice, too, how they refuse to allow you to cling to them. They may allow you to hold on, but never to cling. This can make a cling crab very mad. The freedom-loving crab knows that what is best for one's self is best for everyone.

Once you get over your mad, you can understand why you have to learn more and more, practice more and more, love more and more and how difficult it is to stay free. If you make it back to open water, you will never again allow another crab to cling to you either.

Whatever you want to do in your new ocean, you can do it. If another crab can do it, so can you. If you see a crab you like, ask the crab how it got that way.

You'll find teachers everywhere. Some crabs teach you in books, some teach you in schools, some teach by being an example, some teach you without being asked and some teach by being what you don't want to be.

You'll begin to recognize pain, and you'll have no need to grow barnacles. Barnacles will only slow you down.

Remember that transition is always easier with help, but you'll soon know the way back to the mud all by yourself.

After each rebirth you'll learn about water you've not yet traveled and more about another ocean that's always in front of you.

Love,

Anna

"I never want you to forget the crab stories. You'll be growing the rest of your life, Miss Zoe. Each time you're in emotional pain, remember a crab story. Feel the pain and grow into it.

"When the pain first starts, it will be the most painful. Once it becomes familiar, you'll have some reference. You can add and subtract material of your choice. If the pain continues to repeat itself, you can let your little crab fingers relax and let go."

I said, "Anna, I'm as sad as a comic strip character who was telling his friend about a vacation with his guru — about his fantastic time and all his new knowledge. The friend asked,

'If you are so happy, why are you so sad?' To which he replied, 'I forgot my mantra.'

"Well, Anna, I'll never forget my mantra!"

My eyes were watering; my throat and chest were tight. I backed the car through the heavy sand and turned onto the main highway before I spoke. Anna was very still and exceptionally quiet. I don't remember what either of us said until we got to her home. After I carried her things into the kitchen Anna said, "Until tomorrow, okay?"

End of Eleventh Day with Anna

I drove home and the first thing I did was look at the clay sculpture I'd made for Anna.

About eight inches high, it was the back of a nude woman, sitting, with her arms held straight and extended up and out, slightly above her head and wide apart. Her hands were open and reaching.

The legs were covered with clay, but they were obviously completely extended forward and apart.

I saw her with her back to the beach and the strong wind blowing her hair straight and forward.

An extension — a cloak of clay — is a part of her slightly forward leaning torso.

The cloak along her arms encircle the entire secure, seated sculpture with a flowing whimsical strength.

The front and sides, inside and out, of the graceful cloak is finished like a sea-shell with the edges firmly scalloped.

Looking at it from the back, I could see a well formed woman's body with her head tilting slightly to the right and the elegant draped cloak flaring wide and open.

I loved it until I turned it around.

I had left the front unfinished. I was uncomfortable with the raw, unfinished, nakedness of her insides showing until I related the sculpture to my lessons with Anna.

One of my projections was that the sculpture represented my new flexibility. Now I had a symbolic figure into which I could see my own insides. The cloak represented a cover attached to my "self," to me, to all of me.

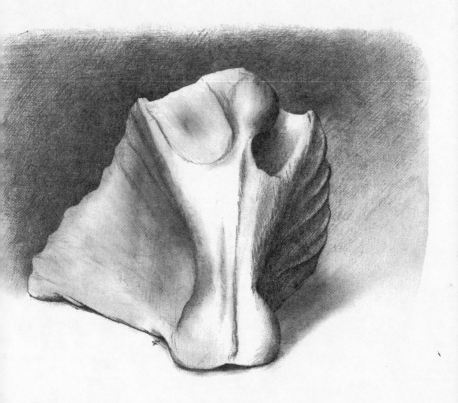

Art by Nolan Skipper

Another projection was that by opening and showing my feelings with Anna, I could be free to be open or closed. I now had a choice. Before Anna, Santa, God and Love, I had no choice; my insides were closed and protected by the same flowing cloak.

My sculpture was like one of the trees, adjusting to the strong wind, leaning forward, firmly seated, yet with a delicate but firmly attached cloak.

I had a negative reaction to the cloak and reluctantly accepted that it represented to me what I once referred to as a Chattel Mortgage Bundle. My bundle, no longer negotiable, was now firmly attached. In the sculpture I could see the work I'd done and all the work yet to be done. However, she appeared to be ready to *let go* all the way to her tiny fingers and claws.

CHAPTER
THIRTEEN

Thursday, December 23, 1982

As soon as I walked in, Anna took her gift from my hands.
I read my note to her aloud while she hugged the sculpture.

Emerson said, '. . . Rings and things are excuses for gifts, the
only true gift is a portion of one's self . . .'
This portion of myself — my gift to you, Anna, is this piece of
unfired clay I named 'Vulnerable' — a word which means to me,
capable of being wounded.

Zoe

Anna examined the sculpture with her magnifying glass
while I waited for her words, "When I feel insecure, I can
snuggle inside her. You named her Vulnerable? Well, she is
that for sure! A little like Jessica — very teachable, wouldn't
you say?"

Anna patted Vulnerable on the head and said, "Keep your
hairstylist, old gal. She's a great one!"

She wanted to walk to the end of the pier to say good-bye.
It was a beautiful cool day with just the perfect amount of

sunshine. We sat on the pier with our feet dangling — gently kicking them together as we talked.

"Anna, I want to know what's fun for you today? What's pleasure to you? What gets you excited?"

"That's the easiest question you've asked me." Her eyes brightened when she said, "I get excited when I see a new student walk by several days in a row. The more days it takes for them to 'let go' and walk down the driveway, the more crab stories I have them read. I always have a new lesson plan because I teach what I need to hear. With that plan one of us is always happy. A new student! Now, that's something to get excited about. Each student has contributed to my notebook.

"You'll be writing to me won't you? I need all the pop psychology you can write."

"Definitely," I promised with a voice full of the love I was feeling.

I reminded her of the story about the tribesmen going across the river late at night and putting a few pebbles in their pockets only to discover later in their journey that the pebbles were diamonds. I held her hand a little tighter and said, "The difference in that story and mine is that I knew from the minute I met you, Anna, that every pebble was a diamond. I'm sad that I can't get more. But I'm glad, so very glad, that I got what I did and that I had the opportunity."

Anna said, "I was thinking about that same little story and about your gift to me. I'm so sad I can't look at Vulnerable and see her with my own eyes. But I'm glad that you gave me something I can hold and feel when I miss you."

"I don't want to leave, Anna. You must be the wisest little old lady on this planet."

We both looked into the water for a long period of time, being silent together. Finally Anna said. "I feel a lot of Isaac Newton's words, 'I do not know what I may appear to the world, but to myself I seem to have been only like a boy playing on the seashore and diverting myself by now and then finding a smoother pebble or a prettier shell than ordinary, while the great ocean of truth lay all undiscovered before me.' "

Santa Claus, God and Love

SUGGESTED READING

Al-Anon Faces Alcoholism, Cornwall Press, 1971.

Bach, Richard, **Illusions,** Dell Publishing, 1977.

Bach, Richard, **Jonathan Livingston Seagull,** MacMillan, 1970.

Bowen, Murray, M. D., **Family Therapy in Clinical Practice,** Jason Aronson, 1978.

Burns, David D., M. D., **Feeling Good,** Signet, 1980.

Fishel, Ruth, **The Journey Within: A Spiritual Path To Recovery,** 1987, **Learning To Live in the Now: 6-Week Personal Plan to Recovery,** 1988, **Time for Joy: Daily Affirmations,** Health Communications, 1988.

Franz, Marie-Louise von, **Projection and Re-collection in Jungian Psychology,** Open Court, 1980.

Grinder and Bandler, **Trance-formations,** Real People Press, 1981.

Jampolsky, Gerald, **Love is Letting Go of Fear,** Bantam Books, 1981.

Jung, Emma, **Animus and Anima,** Spring Publications, 1981.

Keating, Thomas, **Open Mind, Open Heart,** Amity House, 1986.

Kierkegaard, Soren, **The Works of Love,** Harper and Row, 1980.

Lindbergh, Anne Morrow, **Gift From The Sea,** Pantheon, 1955.

Low, Abraham, M. D., **Mental Health Through Will-Training,** 1974.

Mandino, Og, **The Greatest Miracle in the World,** Bantam Books, 1981.

Miller, Joy, **Addictive Relationships: Reclaiming Your Boundaries,** Health Communications, 1989.

Missildine, W. Hugh, M. D., **Your Inner Child of the Past,** Simon & Schuster, 1963.

Salzman, Leon, **Treatment of the Obsessive Personality,** Jason Aronson, 1985.

Shain, Merle, **When Lovers Are Friends,** Bantam Books, 1979.

Smedes, Lewis B., **Love Within Limits,** Wm. B. Eerdmans Publishing, 1979.